Uncovered

The Truth about Honesty and Community

Uncovered

The Truth about Honesty and Community

ROD TUCKER

Kregel
Publications

ISBN 978-0-8254-4334-3

Printed in the United States of America
14 15 16 17 18 / 5 4 3 2 1

To Beautiful Anna Joy.
You are the most amazing bride I could
have ever imagined.

CONTENTS

HOMELESS IN THE PARK

Greg was visiting a fund-raiser for the homeless. It was a brisk fall afternoon at a park in the middle of the city in which he lived, and a large number of churches were participating. The smell of cold weather approaching was prevalent. Each church was raising money and, at the end of the day, would pool their funds with the other churches in an effort to fight homelessness for the winter in Greg's city. Everyone was wearing bright yellow T-shirts to show they were all on the same team, that they were combating homelessness together. That is, everyone except Greg in his denim jacket and black jeans.

As he walked through the crowd Greg could see the busy people scurrying about, encouraging each other in their passionate endeavors to bring change to this fallen world. The people were incredibly focused on what they were doing, fighting homelessness, and very little was able to distract them from the goals of the day. Not even Greg.

As he moved through the sea of people, they spread apart as if he were Moses himself commanding the waves to separate so he might pass. Not one of them looked him in the eye, not one of them said

11

hello, not one of them noticed Greg's existence as a human being in their midst. A human being made in the image of God. The people were too busy. They only saw themselves. And the irony of it all was that Greg was one of the homeless for whom these people said they were fighting. But as he passed, he went unacknowledged, unaccepted, and unseen.

When I first heard Greg's story from my friends as we were eating dinner in downtown Kalamazoo, Michigan, I laughed. But when Tim and Ellen assured me the story was very real, I was shaken. Tim and Ellen were there and they had witnessed Greg's experience. They were not part of the fund-raising event itself, but as they observed the phenomenon of a homeless man invisibly passing through a church crowd so consumed by its own ministry, they became enraged by the injustice that was occurring. My friends were angry. Greg was hurt.

He did meet eyes with Tim and Ellen for an instant. Greg looked at them and they looked back as if to apologize for all the hurt that others' good intentions had caused him. They were the only people who had noticed him in the crowd. Ellen told me afterward she had the sense that Greg was like Jesus. We talked about the idea that maybe what the people in the crowd that day really missed out on, by not acknowledging Greg, was quite possibly the God who had taken the time to come into their presence, to be with them. But because they were so caught up in themselves, and attempting to be "better Christians" by doing what they felt was ministry, they never noticed Him walking in their midst.

This idea comes from Matthew 25:31–46, where we read that upon Jesus' second return He will separate the nations by showing how

He in fact was the hungry, thirsty, and naked of the world. Some people welcomed Him into their lives and others did not. To those who did, Jesus claims to know them, and to those who did not, He says, "Whatever you did not do for one of the least of these, you did not do for me."[1] The reasons to welcome or not welcome Jesus into one's life may vary, but the idea that Jesus is the hurting person in these people's lives is unavoidable.

Isn't that quite the story? The God of the universe comes to our world, walks among us, and we do not even notice He is here. I wonder how this story ends. For now, it is the story of people who have become so caught up in themselves that they cannot see past their own reflection in a mirror. This is the story of people who do not love because they are blind to the broken who pass by without rest, without comfort, and without grace. This is our story.

In the pages that follow, you will find more of the problem of dishonesty and living in the dark, and you will be invited into a deeper conversation as to how we can become communities that engage the kingdom of God authentically through honesty. My hope is that as you read this book, you will be inspired to live a life of honesty . . . and in doing so find the grace and freedom to engage the hurting of this world who go unnoticed.

Before we get going, let me first tell you a failing of mine. Several years ago I noticed, as you probably did too, that people began surgically injecting themselves with plastic-like substances to appear more beautiful. After they had done this they were still the same, but their hope apparently was that people's perception of them might change. Maybe people would see them as more sexually attractive. Maybe others would desire them in more ways than they had before surgery. The bottom line was that there was a twisting of reality. The fake overwhelmed the real. I watched as this mentality overtook the media and had us all wanting to appear different, wanting to seem better, even if we knew it was fake. This way of thinking had become so much larger than plastic surgery. It had impacted the way we thought about everything, including our own spirituality. When I eventually realized how crazy this is, I wondered why this mentality of faking and pretending to be someone I was not was so easily acceptable to me. Why didn't I fight it? Then the truth hit me. I didn't learn this way of thinking and acting and pretending I was better than I was from the strip in Las Vegas or Amsterdam or Bourbon Street in New Orleans or even MTV. I learned it in church.

The point of this little self-disclosure is that this book is a process. It begins with the topic of honesty as an individual lifestyle and then progresses through its three parts into what this means for Christian community. The end result is hopefully a picture of the body of Christ spending less time and energy focused selfishly on itself, and more time and energy spent paying attention to the Jesuses of this world. The ones who are waiting for us to come to them with grace, peace, hugs, acceptance, cold water, clothing, or food.

This book is meant to be read in its entirety as it introduces, comments upon, and invites others into a dialogue that needs to be had in Christian community. I thank you for picking this book up, and I hope we can both learn to embrace honesty, like a kiss on the lips,[2] and then together shift away from this plastic mentality of church and toward genuine fellowship.

ACKNOWLEDGMENTS

Creative Consulting: Thomas Wrench, thomaswrench.com

Who Rod is following:

Anna Joy Tucker: considergrace.com

Brian Fraaza: brianfraaza.com

Special Thanks: Everyone I love, and everyone who loves me. My family is amazing: Dad, Mom, Lisa, Doug, Christie, Jay, Kelly, Scott, Michael, Maddox, Kyla, Mimi, Lindy, Carol, Tim, Kristi, Mary, Xander, and beautiful Anna Joy. Thanks for loving me so much. A lot of people read this book and gave me feedback. I am incredibly thankful for this also. To begin remembering those names would be amazingly difficult, but I can try: Anna, Christie, Elizabeth, Peter, Thomas, Kayli, Jon, Molly, Mom (Diane), Dad (Craig), Elisha, Len, Kevin, Kati, Brian, Kent, Dan, Scott, Drew, Alisha, Erica, Lindy, Carol, Wil, Rob, Tim, Kristi, Judy, Bekah, Peter, Travis, Emily, Dennis, and Dori. Tim and Anna, thanks for going through it twice. Thank you everyone for being a part of my life, and thank you for teaching me, inspiring me, and allowing me to live in honesty. To begin listing names of friends who impact my life undoubtedly means that someone may accidentally get left out, and we wouldn't want that.

Part 1

ME, MYSELF, AND HONESTY

LIKE A KISS ON THE LIPS

*But if we are living in the light, as God is in the light,
then we have fellowship with each other, and the
blood of Jesus, his Son, cleanses us from all sin.*

1 John 1:7 NLT

An honest answer is like a kiss on the lips.

Proverbs 24:26

My first kiss was in a car, at night, in the dark. My lips smashed up against my girlfriend's and although I was expecting something more meaningful, all I felt was wet, squishy lips. It was one of the more awkward moments I have ever experienced. Sometime later I met my wife, Anna, and now there are no awkward kisses. Every kiss is given and received with grace. Yes, kissing is still vulnerable, but kissing the one you love is magical. *Honesty is like kissing.* Honesty is an introduction to something much more powerful and intimate: relationships bred by transparency.

When we live in darkness, things cannot be seen. But when we live in the light, everything becomes visible. This verse from 1 John in the Bible points to the fellowship, healing, and forgiveness that can occur when things are out in the open, when we choose to live honestly. This kind of living is what 1 John 1:7 calls "walking in the light."

At first, walking and living in the light is awkward. Questions such as, "How are people going to receive me?" parade through our thoughts, and many times even keep us from living transparently with others. But once we begin to take those steps—to make honest living a lifestyle—we begin to enjoy the outcome. We feel accepted. Like a first kiss, honest living can feel awkward at first; but if embraced purely, it can eventually lead to an unparalleled wholeness and oneness, both in the individual and among the community.

Honesty can propel us perpetually into a realm of existence where we can begin to know others in deep ways. Ways that allow us to care about others. Maybe even care for others like Jesus cares for us. We are not called to live for ourselves. We are not called to focus on ourselves. We are called to die to ourselves and, through this death, love other people. Second Corinthians 5:15 says, "And he died for all, that those who live should no longer live for themselves but for him who died for them and was raised again." If we know anything from the heart of the gospel of Jesus Christ, it is this: when we die so others might live, we get resurrected. This is what Jesus did, and we have the opportunity to share in this love through our lives. We experience intimacy, grace, and most of all, an ability to see others in their circumstances instead of only ourselves. We get to experience life as it is truly meant to be lived.[1] This is grace.

With honesty comes grace; and honesty is the doorway to transformation, a catalyst into communal intimacy. Think about Jesus' parable of two men praying in Luke 18:10. One man, a Pharisee, prayed about himself in front of God. He was prideful, fake, and clearly not living in the light. The other man, a tax collector, humbled himself, became transparent, and ultimately received mercy. This parable provides a powerful image of community centered on Jesus. In the same way the tax collector was humble and honest and received God's mercy, we are to humble ourselves before God and each other so that we can be exalted and also exalt each other. Honesty brings grace when there are people willing to extend God's grace after receiving honesty. Galatians 6:2–3 says, "Carry each other's burdens, and in this way you will fulfill the law of Christ. If anyone thinks they are something when they are not, they deceive themselves." Communal intimacy is embraced best when people lay themselves bare before each other and in return are accepted by the transformative grace of Jesus. When we live transparently, everything changes, and that is the point.

Individual Reflection / Group Discussion

How is honesty like kissing?

Have you ever felt the need to hide from others instead of living in the light? Why?

2

SELF-PROTECTION

When I was a junior in college, I took a trip to visit my sister, Kelly, in Michigan. She worked at a college ministry called The Gathering, on the campus of Western Michigan University. I always enjoyed going to see Kelly because I was able to participate in all of the weekend retreats, some of the small group leadership meetings, and the Sunday evening main event. On this specific occasion—and I was not sure exactly how the circumstance designed itself—I found myself sitting in a one-on-one meeting with one of the individuals involved in the ministry.

Eventually we ended up talking about sexual sin and lust and how it is a difficult topic among males. He said he knew a number of men dealing with the temptation to have sex outside of marriage, relationship problems, and the struggle with pornography. Being only twenty years old and having a limited experience with talking to others about such issues, I decided to share some of my ideas regarding these topics.

I began by stating that sexuality was an intense topic and there was a definite need for discussion. I related that I did have some experience with sexual issues, and had shared some of what I had learned through my own experiences with others in order to help them heal. I was trying to talk about honesty. He nodded his head in agreement, giving me even more confidence to speak. And so I continued: "I tell guys I used to struggle with pornography, and I think it helps them be honest with me." His response was different than I expected: "Why not instead of saying 'I *used to*,' say, 'I *do* struggle with pornography'?" Simply put, he had caught me in a lie. While I was *somewhat* honest (in being willing to declare a struggle), I was dishonest in my intent. Instead of being open and honest with God, myself, and others, I was saying, "I am not as bad as the next guy . . . I have overcome."

The truth was, like many other men (and women), I struggled with visual temptation. Some days I did great resisting and some days I did not, but I was evasive about my full struggle. To justify my lack of honesty I used a time line measuring how long I could go without sinning. I was so focused on how "successful" I was in overcoming my sexual sin that I was often unable to have grace for myself. Without grace, I became too self-focused—judging my own wins and losses—and was therefore forced to judge those around me who struggled with the exact same issues, and consequently was unable to extend authentic grace.

Sexual struggles are common among people everywhere today. Paul writes in 1 Corinthians, "No temptation has overtaken you except what is common to mankind."[1] The problem is many of us have not chosen to be honest about the extent of our weaknesses. Instead we have chosen to minimize our secret sins or use "past-tense language" to cover our shame, sending the message that sin is an old issue for us. At least this is how I was living. I was definitely not agreeing with Paul's words in Romans:

> I do not understand what I do. For what I want
> to do I do not do, but what I hate I do. And if I
> do what I do not want to do, I agree that the law
> is good. As it is, it is no longer I myself who do it,
> but it is sin living in me. For I know that good itself
> does not dwell in me, that is, in my sinful nature.
> For I have the desire to do what is good, but I can-
> not carry it out. For I do not do the good I want
> to do, but the evil I do not want to do—this I keep
> on doing.[2]

I had chosen not to be honest with myself at all, much less with someone who could help me find greater freedom. Rather, in order to keep up the appearance of spiritual health, I had faked that I no longer struggled with pornography. I spoke using the past tense, as if sin was only in my past. I had told myself I could speak like this because I had experienced a short time span of not looking at pornography. No matter how I manipulated my words, I lied to myself and to my friend.

We claim that we, as individuals, have overcome sin, when sin is something only Jesus can overcome, and that we are now qualified to judge others who do not overcome on their own. All the while, Jesus tells us to take the planks out of our own eyes before we even consider looking at another's sin.[3] We are lying to each other and ourselves. We have exchanged true honesty for self-protection.

We protect ourselves from the rejection we believe we are sure to receive if others really see what's inside. So we fake it. For instance, if visitors are headed to our home with little notice, we will undoubtedly take a quick moment to shove all of our excess junk into drawers and make our house *appear* as though it is cleaner than it truly is. In doing so we preserve our home façade, and the visitors go home feeling as though they need to make their homes as tidy and as nice as ours. This façade as a lifestyle could easily turn into a vicious cycle; and it does, both in our homes and in our lives. John Burke said it best when he wrote: "If you want to pretend you have no struggles, no problems, no sins, no wounds, then go play that game somewhere else, because that's not real."[4]

Individual Reflection / Group Discussion

Do you feel it is ever appropriate to not be totally honest about the sin in your life? Why or why not?

Have you ever spoken about your sin in a past tense language when it was not past tense in your life? Why do you think you did that?

3

SEWING, HIDING, AND BLAMING

In Genesis chapter 3, three distinct actions take place after Adam and Eve sin.[1] First, they sew fig leaves to cover their exposed parts, of which they are suddenly ashamed. Adam and Eve do not want anyone else to see that they are naked. Second, they hide because their coverings do not work, and they now believe every part of them needs to be hidden from sight. Adam and Eve feel that if God sees them they might be revealed for who they truly are, which is (precisely) naked, vulnerable, and now ashamed. Third, Adam and Eve blame each other and the serpent for their sin instead of owning up to their choices, thus missing out on the freedom and forgiveness that come from confession. As 1 John 1:9 says, "If we confess our sins, he is faithful and just and will forgive us our sins and purify us from all unrighteousness." Confession and purification go together and help us, by grace, to think clearly after sin has brought confusion to our minds. This is one of the purposes of forgiveness. We learn that we do not have to earn our way back into right relationship. We can be forgiven and purified through confession.

Sewing, hiding, and blaming are tactics we have all used at one time or another. For most of us, sewing comes first. We try to cover our sin and pretend everything is okay. We want others to not notice us for the guilt and shame we feel on the inside. Second, we realize that our ability to sew a good covering or pretend like everything is fine after we have sinned has fallen incredibly short of our goal and is not doing the job effectively. Simply put, we still feel awful and judged whether people have noticed our fakeness or not. So we hide. We hide because we are no good at pretending, and hiding seems to be the best way to make sure no one else sees our junk. In sewing, we cover up our "shameful" parts, and in hiding we cover up everything. Both sewing and hiding come from the fear of being seen fully or known.

I have a friend who says she will never come to church because "the church is a bunch of hypocrites," as she puts it. What I know about my friend is that, when she was a little girl growing up in church, she saw more pretending and faking than she could stomach. People would put on their Sunday best and head to church, unwilling to admit any junk in their lives. My friend learned this behavior as well, but sooner than many of the other people in her church, she realized how fake this made her feel. So she quit. She quit going to church, which maybe was the right move for her at the time. But she also quit pursuing authentic relationships. Somewhere along the line, because of her experience, my friend began to believe Christianity was simply a religion for pretenders, and she wanted nothing to do with it. For my friend, sewing fig leaves led quickly to hiding from anything that had the potential to bring grace her way. She became afraid of being seen and judged, and now she stands at a distance and blames.

I also know a man who is still pretending, sewing figurative fig leaves to this day. Everyone around him knows what he is doing. He and I have never sat down and had a conversation about the junk in his life because he will not allow it. However, every Sunday morning he shows up with a smile on his face and a "God is good" to everyone he meets. People have asked him to talk. People have asked him to share. He gives the same response almost every time. A smile and a "God is good."

I think my friend who does not go to church anymore got fed up with people like the man who is still sewing fig leaves today. The problem is, neither of them will receive any kind of healing in their lives until they can stop, take an honest look at themselves, and open up to someone or a community who will have grace for them.

I was sewing fig leaves when I was pretending that I "used to" struggle with pornography. The way I chose to phrase my struggle made me feel as though I was either not *fully* naked or at least covered enough so others could not see me as I truly was. And in a sense I was blaming too, because pointing the finger and talking about others' sin was my attempt to keep the focus off of me.

Blaming can sometimes be as subtle as using what seem to be positive slogans, such as "Hate the sin, love the sinner." Phrases like this justify pointing the finger and taking the focus off of ourselves. We do not want to be seen with our junk, so we point out other people's junk and turn the focus onto them. We reason, if everyone is looking at another person, no one is looking at me. Ultimately, these kinds of statements, "Hate the sin, love the sinner" do nothing more than allow for one group of people, many times Christian communities, to appear righteous and holy (right) and the marginalized to be viewed as offensive (wrong). It does not matter how correct what we believe we are saying is. Blaming is blaming. For some reason we always have to make ourselves look and feel like the good guy.

I have heard several different popular preachers take highly judgmental stances on topics such as homosexuality, pornography, and marriage. I have also seen these same preachers, years later, be found out for having a secret homosexual relationship, a pornography addiction, and even an extramarital affair. These people were blaming, and they did an effective job of shifting the focus off of themselves and onto others. But in the end, these preachers, too, were uncovered.

Adam and Eve did the same thing when they pointed in each other's direction, casting blame for their own wrongdoing. In reality all of this sewing, hiding, and blaming resulted from shame, from Adam and Eve looking at each of their own bodies and believing the lie that there was something wrong with them.

I remember coming to church as a college student, believing there was something wrong with me, and wearing the disguise of sinless perfection. I would have never claimed to be sinless had someone asked, but my manipulative language always pointed to how sin, especially pornography, was an old issue for me. I talked as though I had attained such a high spiritual level that I had developed some sort of force field that kept most, if not all, twisted sexual thoughts out of my head. Ultimately, this fake moral living kept me from experiencing true freedom for years.

I had also chosen to hide from others rather than search for the most truthful and sincere relationships I could build. I blamed others and compared sins as if I were measuring them on some sort of divine Richter scale instead of looking to Jesus, who took all of my inadequacies and shame so that I might look upon others and myself with gracious eyes. I never gave honesty a true chance. I never allowed living in the light to become a lifestyle, enabling me to move into greater freedom. It was not until years later that I finally entered into authentically transparent relationships which allowed me to experience grace and healing I could have never found on my own.

A word to some of you who may have given honesty a momentary chance, and instead of being received with grace, were ridiculed and rejected—while I understand the choice to be honest does not result in gracious community every single time without fail, I do know that honesty must become an ongoing lifestyle in order for us to experience true grace and acceptance. This is not something we can try once or twice and then give up completely. Honesty must be allowed to prove itself as true and good, as the building blocks for accepting and healthy relationships. But almost always, a lifestyle of honesty will take perseverance. Believe me, I know. Not everyone is always gracefully accepting. In the same light, if we want to experience grace-filled community, we need to be gracious to others who are willing to take the first step of honesty.

There is a wonderful conversation in *The Velveteen Rabbit*, a children's novel by Margery Williams, that helps illustrate my point almost perfectly. This story is a beautiful encounter between toys in a child's playroom. The toys want to be real, and in many ways have even created hierarchies so they might know who is real and who is not. The conversation goes like this:

> "What is REAL?" asked the Rabbit one day, when they were lying side by side near the nursery fender, before Nana came to tidy the room. "Does it mean having things that buzz inside you and a stick-out handle?"

"Real isn't how you are made," said the Skin Horse. "It's a thing that happens to you. When a child loves you for a long, long time, not just to play with, but REALLY loves you, then you become Real."

"Does it hurt?" asked the Rabbit.

"Sometimes," said the Skin Horse, for he was always truthful. "When you are Real you don't mind being hurt."

"Does it happen all at once, like being wound up," he asked, "or bit by bit?"

"It doesn't happen all at once," said the Skin Horse. "You become. It takes a long time. That's why it doesn't often happen to people who break easily, or have sharp edges, or who have to be carefully kept. Generally, by the time you are Real, most of your hair has been loved off, and your eyes drop out and you get loose in the joints and very shabby. But these things don't matter at all, because once you are Real you can't be ugly, except to people who don't understand."[2]

To have an open and honest relationship with God and others in true community is to be *real*. This is a place where no one is ugly, because everyone is the same. We are all sinners, and by the grace of God through Christ we who through faith come and surrender to Him have been made acceptable, desirable, and pure. Some may understand this and others may not, but this is not the point.

The point is that real and honest relationships have a grace that far outweighs any temptation to be perfect or to fake perfection. This is what God has made available to us through Jesus. All sinners—whether redeemed or not yet—are invited and welcome to come and receive this grace by which God makes us become real.

Honesty is a place where the true nature of Christ and humanity collide. The gospel of Jesus redirects us to confess our sins, humble ourselves before God and others, and receive grace. From there, rather than trying to fix ourselves, we can walk confidently—in Christ's perfection—into a world that would much rather have us bring restoration to those in need than to spend our time maintaining our own images.

Individual Reflection / Group Discussion

Can you give an example of sewing/hiding/blaming from your own life?

What are ways you have faked being a "good Christian"?

4

KNOWING AND BEING KNOWN

When Adam and Eve first saw each other in the garden of Eden we know they were naked and not ashamed. I can imagine they viewed and thought of each other as beings created in the image of God, with no needed accessories. Then after they had sinned, Adam and Eve realized they were naked and became ashamed. They tried to become something they were not and could never be: because of their sin, they realized that they did not measure up, and the lie was that somehow their imperfection was not okay.

When Adam and Eve realized they were naked, they became aware of the physical and realized more than a lack of covering. Adam and Eve realized they did not measure up to God. I now begin to understand why God did not want Adam and Eve eating from the tree of knowledge in the first place. The Creator of the universe knew who He was, and He did not need to prove Himself to anyone. However, when Adam and Eve tried to become like God—believing the lie that they deserved such knowledge—they found they did not measure up and were in fact naked in every way. Later in history, the Levitical Law became the measuring stick; but humankind, misinterpreting the ultimate goal of grace, decided they would try to "measure up" again on their own.

Throughout Scripture and throughout our lives we can see a common thread—there is an Enemy (the serpent, Satan, the Devil, the Thief, and so on) who is fighting against humans.[1] Human beings are the only creation of God made in His image.[2] Since the Enemy is in fact an enemy of God and cannot be in God's image, this leads him to do everything in his power to dehumanize us. John 10:10 says, "The thief comes only to steal and kill and destroy." First, he tempts us to pursue perfection, like God, having a flawless appearance, unparalleled success, and enviable moral character. Second, we attempt to achieve perfection, and in failing to do so, he is able to convince us we are less than human. This invites the lie that we are animals: dirty, primitive, and unworthy of meaningful relationships. This is exactly what the serpent did with Adam and Eve in Genesis 3, and we see this message mirrored in the culture around us through sexual immorality, eating disorders, shame, guilt, and addictions. We then try harder to become perfect, oftentimes using the old ways that got us into trouble in the first place, and this vicious cycle continues, keeping our focus continually on ourselves.

In a spiritual sense, we try to attain holiness through a sinless life. The results are the same. We fail to achieve perfection, and ultimately end up feeling useless in the kingdom of God. Sin, or the attempt to not sin by overcoming a specific struggle, becomes our focus instead of honest living, giving and receiving grace, and being Christ to other people.

The true issue is not the *struggle* with sin. Rather, the issue is our attempt to protect a distorted image of ourselves and somehow "measure up" through inauthentic moral living, instead of being open and honest with God and fellow members of Christ's body.

We see this spiritual idea of measuring up play out in a physical way through the emphasis our culture places on physical appearance. Men and women are evidently supposed to look a certain way. Men are supposed to have all the right muscles, in all the right places, all the time. Even women who just had a child many times go through a stage of depression because they think that since the baby is here, everything is supposed to go back to normal, and physically they are supposed to look as they once did. This is absurd, and it is also a lie that we too can be unchanging in nature, like God. Too many of us eat from that tree far too often.

However, when two people decide that they, above all else, desire to love and be with each other for the rest of their earthly lives, they not only get married but they also consummate their marriage by making passionate love. They do not just have sex. These people make love.

I am sure that many brides and grooms dreadfully look forward to the moment of nakedness and honesty on their wedding night. If the two have never seen each other naked before, I imagine the girl questioning whether or not her husband will think she is beautiful. In the same way, I imagine the guy wondering if he can be enough for his wife. The question is posed: *will my spouse still be attracted to me after I am seen naked?*

A few years ago my friends Jared and Jessica asked this question in a rather intentional way. Jessica went to tanning salons. She dieted.

Jared started a regular routine of weightlifting. For the first time in months they both began to watch what they ate. As their confidence went up in what they were doing to make themselves acceptable to the other, their fears of being unattractive also heightened. But this did not stop my friends from working hard on their individual appearances. Why? Because they wanted to make sure the other found them attractive on their wedding night. They wanted to try to *measure up*.

But measuring up is not the goal of true sex at all. And a healthy understanding of sex has huge implications for our understanding of honesty and grace. For example, when Anna and I got married we were more in love than ever before, and sex became an expression of how much we loved each other. I remember our wedding night and how in the moment Anna was totally revealed to me, I stressed to her how wonderful and beautiful she was. In response— because she thought the same about me as I did of her—Anna received my nakedness unconditionally with a grace that made me feel completely accepted and loved.

Sex reveals some of our most intimate fears and encourages us to transcend our own, sometimes shameful, understanding of ourselves and place our hearts into the judgment and approval of another's eyes. And when this "oneness" is reached in the context of marriage, the freedom can be exponential. To be known fully and be accepted fully, at the same time, is to be set free. Knowing this we can agree with God, when we are *known* by Him in the most intimate ways, that we know the truth and the truth has set us free.[3] We certainly have a gracious God since He would allow us to get back to a place of being naked and unashamed, through marriage.

One of my mentors (who is in his later years) told me his wife is more attractive to him now than the day they got married, and I know he was talking about something more than physical appearance. For my mentor, true love extended beyond a love for the physical only; and he knew, as his marriage reached a point of longevity, his relationship with his wife would only become stronger. When he told me this I wanted the exact same intimacy with my wife.

The truth is, marriage is one of the better metaphors for understanding what kind of relationship God desires with us. Ultimately, He does call us His bride. But what is most intriguing to me is that the intimacy marriage offers is rooted in being laid totally bare and naked, and being unashamed regardless. Sure, our culture and sin tries to twist this back into a place of shame, but what is being offered here through marital intimacy is an opportunity to be known and to know, to be seen and to see, to have grace for and receive grace from another whom we love. If you ask me, this all sounds a lot like I John 1:7: "But if we walk in the light, as he is in the light, we have fellowship with one another, and the blood of Jesus, his Son, purifies us from all sin."

God asks us to look at ourselves, and then no matter what fears, shame, or guilt we have, open ourselves completely up to Him. He desires to see, have, and experience us for all we truly are. I think this understanding of Jesus is essential and beautiful, and it comes full circle with Psalm 139 when David writes, "Search me, God, and know my heart; test me and know my anxious thoughts. See if there is any offensive way in me, and lead me in the way everlasting."[4]

Individual Reflection / Group Discussion

In what ways have you tried to "measure up" to some particular standard?

What are the risks/benefits from using the words of David, "Search me and know me" in your relationship with God?

5

ALCOHOLICS ANONYMOUS

During the middle of my college years I was sitting in my professor's office eyeing his small library of religion, philosophy, and other interesting books (all of which seemed far too intelligent for me to even touch), when I noticed a blue book titled *Alcoholics Anonymous*. The title of the book was intriguing to me because as a young boy I had grown up attending Alcoholics Anonymous meetings with my parents yet I had never heard of this book. Most times I was given the opportunity to sit in on these meetings, but other times I would play outside with a babysitter.

When not attending the actual meetings, it was definitely a unique experience to hang out with children who had family situations a lot like myself. We all knew our parents were struggling with or had previously struggled with alcohol, drugs, codependency, or any number of other coping mechanisms used to deal with shame and pain. We also all knew alcohol, as cunning and deceptive as it was, had in some way or another affected us as children of alcoholics. We all shared in the tendency to feel like our family was screwed up, and other families who were not in attendance were not. Little did we know that our parents had embarked upon a journey of unparalleled success. They were being honest with each other, and

in so doing learning that in this world there really are no super individuals. We are all the same.

As I Corinthians 10:13 says, "No temptation has overtaken you
except what is common to mankind." We are all human. We all
struggle, and when we are honest we can know we are not the
only ones who do. I recalled all of this while sitting in my professor's
office, and I suddenly had the strongest urge to go to my mother
and tell her about this book. The professor lent me his copy.

On the way home I had the opportunity to read some of the book,
and discovered that it was mainly a collection of stories dealing with
people's attempts to be honest and heal from the pain of alcohol
abuse. This included quitting drinking altogether. But some stories
told of much deeper, root causes of the dysfunction in their lives.
Many of the stories involved children who grew up with alcoholic
parents, and as a result became alcoholics themselves in coping with
their past experiences. However, in my reading I came to a chapter
titled "How It Works," and I quickly began to understand why my
parents were doing as well as they were—at that time clean and
sober for more than twenty-five years.

I read the chapter, and after arriving home, I quickly pulled the book
out of my bag and asked my mom if I could read something to her.
I was excited to share something refreshing with my mom, something that let her know I understood what was happening in the
Alcoholics Anonymous meetings I attended with her as a child. I
felt like it was going to be one of those moments when my mother
and I understood each other in a greater light. She didn't know
what I was going to read, so we both sat down in the living room,
and I began to unravel the truth in the book. My lips were clinging

to every word as I read to my mom. I wanted her to feel the same impact I had felt when I first discovered this book. With much excitement I made sure I enunciated perfectly.

I read approximately one and a half sentences before my mother interrupted me by quoting, in its entirety, the rest of the beginning of the chapter. I sat in silence and awe as my mother spoke as though she had memorized something out of the Bible. I did not know what to say. I felt like crying. There was something about what my mother quoted that made perfect sense. What I was just hearing and discovering now had impacted my mother in a similar way years earlier. The moment felt holy. Like when God says He is the Beginning and the End, I had stumbled across something that, for my family, transcended time.[1] It was almost as if three different people from three different times—the writer, myself, and my mom—had collided in the same moment and had somehow reached the same conclusions about life and honesty and what it means to say that we are truly free. This is a small portion of what my mother quoted:

> Rarely have we seen a person fail who has thoroughly followed our path. Those who do not recover are people who cannot or will not completely give themselves to this simple program, usually men and women who are constitutionally incapable of being honest with themselves.[2]

A great realization came over me that day when I finished talking with my mom about Alcoholics Anonymous. I had grown up attending AA meetings with my parents, and was able to witness firsthand the pursuit and experience of both healing and health. I also grew up regularly attending church. What I saw as a child, but did not recognize until I was older, was that although both AA and church offer a freedom from various forms of bondage, both physical and spiritual, only one of them allowed for a transparency that inspired community and true healing. Our culture—and especially our church—has the tendency to tag those who are struggling and honest about their struggles as some kind of freaks, or people who cannot pull themselves together. Preachers constantly preach about deliverance under the premise that if you are not being delivered then you are either living in sin or lacking the adequate faith to allow God to pull you from your miry pit. This is not right, and judgment is not why Jesus came to us. In fact, His reasoning for coming is very much the opposite.

Individual Reflection / Group Discussion

Some say that being honest with oneself is 50 percent of the way to healing. Do you agree? Why or why not?

Have you ever been in a community like AA that modeled and rewarded total honesty? What was your experience like?

DARKNESS AND LIGHT

Personally, I am beginning to believe that people who fight to be honest are actually learning to be more like Jesus than all of the other people who seem to spend their time either sewing leaves to cover their faults, hiding from the truth, or blaming others and saying things like, "Well at least I am not like him!" Striving to be honest, as opposed to striving to be perfect, confronts the shame and reveals its deception. There are no shadows in the light. There is a big difference between pushing ourselves to be perfect and making a choice to live in honesty.

First John 1:5–10 talks about the importance of the choice:

> This is the message we have heard from him and declare to you: God is light; in him there is no darkness at all. If we claim to have fellowship with him and yet walk in the darkness, we lie and do not live out the truth. But if we walk in the light, as he is in the light, we have fellowship with one another, and the blood of Jesus, his Son, purifies us from all sin.
>
> If we claim to be without sin, we deceive ourselves and the truth is not in us. If we confess our sins, he

> is faithful and just and will forgive us our sins and
> purify us from all unrighteousness. If we claim we
> have not sinned, we make him out to be a liar and
> his word is not in us.

I used to think that living in the light meant living without sin. I suppose I believed this after hearing preacher after preacher say that we must get out of darkness through daily devotions, prayer, and (the big kicker) avoiding sin. Of course the problem with this theology is that humans do sin, and ultimately we cannot avoid it. To say that we do not sin, or that we are without sin, even if it is for nothing more than a brief moment, makes God "out to be a liar and his word is not in us."[1] Therefore, choosing to live in the light must mean something more than simply the act of not sinning. A key aspect of choosing to live in the light is honesty, and I am beginning to believe that many other interpretations of this verse pile more dos and don'ts onto our already superfluous list of rules and regulations.

If we live in honesty, we will have fellowship with each other. From the beginning of time in Genesis chapter 1, God has been speaking things into existence. Basically, when God says it, it happens. So when the Holy Spirit, through John, says, "If we walk in the light, as he is in the light, we have fellowship with one another," we can believe that this is true. It does not say we *might* have fellowship, it says we *have* fellowship. This is because when we do choose to live this way, as a result, we are also able to unconditionally receive others with grace and love. For those who live in God's light, fellowship naturally *happens*. However, we must remember, again, that living in the light is far different than giving honesty a one-time chance or a test run. Living in the light is a lifestyle.

James 5:16 says that we are to confess our sins to each other and in turn pray for each other, and the end result will be healing. In an interview with Dr. James Dobson, Ted Bundy, a convicted serial killer on death row, told of a pornography addiction that started his spiral toward further depravity. He said, "I led a normal life, except for this one, small but very potent and destructive segment that I kept very secret and close to myself."[2] For Ted, pornography kept in secret led to extreme violence toward women.[3] I wonder what might have happened to Ted had he been honest with someone early on about his struggle with pornography. Sin likes to hide in the secret shadows of our lives so it can whisper the lie that we are the only one who struggles or that no one will ever understand our struggle. In this way sin can grow and deepen in our hearts, as long as we keep it in the dark.

I wonder if Adam and Eve ran away together and manufactured their elaborately designed fig leaf clothing as a team. Right after they had first sinned, I imagine that they each went their separate ways and individually piled leaves on top of what they thought were their shameful bodies, not wanting the other to see them naked. I also wonder what would have happened had they been honest with God and each other in order to be healed. Either way, sin stayed in the shadows for Adam and Eve. And because they may have gone about it by themselves, it was far easier to hide.

Individual Reflection / Group Discussion

How are people who aim to be honest and transparent like Jesus?

What is the difference between living transparently with others and trying to find healing on your own?

7

"AT LEAST I'M NOT . . ."

When I was in college I had a Christian friend who decided that she was homosexual. Not only that, this epiphany came with a realization that she had (supposedly) been homosexual her entire life, and had somehow been suppressing the feelings of attraction to the same sex until the struggle became too difficult to fight. So she came out of the closet. She said that "coming out" was freeing for her; and that contrary to popular Christian opinion, she felt no further from God spiritually.

When she first told me this, I was taken aback and did not know how to react to my friend . . . or whether or not I should even call her my friend! I thought I had read somewhere in the Bible (I Cor. 5:5) that I was supposed to completely end all communication with my friend and turn her over to Satan. After I remembered the scenario surrounding that particular passage (and confirmed that my friend was not sleeping with her father's wife), I decided that I needed to react in a different way than my initial misunderstanding of Scripture had instructed. In that moment I decided to love my friend and not condemn her based on her actions, even if I felt they were wrong. Instead, I decided to look at her as no different from myself, as someone who was also human and who was slowly—through the healing work of Jesus—being reconciled to God. I remembered Romans 3:23–24, which says, "for all have sinned and fall short of the glory of God, and all are justified freely by his grace through the redemption that came by Christ Jesus." In that moment I realized that we were both imperfect, and no matter what anyone else had to say, because we both knew Jesus, we were both covered by the grace of our Father and nothing could separate us from what Christ had accomplished for us on the cross.[1]

I think that my original, irrational, and unbiblical shaming of those struggling with (or embracing) homosexuality began with a deeper-rooted shame of myself than I knew at the time. Just like Adam and Eve being found naked in the garden after they had first sinned, I found myself in a similar place as I began to understand my own sexuality. If I had a lustful thought or looked at pornography I would always feel ashamed. Then I would remember that these sexual feelings were natural, and I would judge others and console myself by looking in the mirror and saying, "Well, at least I'm not gay." I was once again shifting the attention, in my own mind, off of my own sin and onto others. *Blaming.*

When I read in Genesis 3 about Adam and Eve in the garden of Eden, and notice that at first they tried to fix themselves (or at least cover their nakedness) by sewing fig leaves, I find it amusing that they would choose plant matter—something that easily withers away within a short time. This either proves that Adam and Eve truly were primitive, or that they were quickly and desperately scrounging around for whatever covering they could find . . . anything to make themselves not feel so bad about their choices. When this covering did not work, they both thought that it might be a good idea to hide. So they did, and soon discovered that one cannot, for the sake of all that is good, hide from God Almighty. He will find you. Even more than that, God will then ask you why in the world, literally, you were hiding, and who gave you this stupid idea in the first place. At this point Adam and Eve, like me, chose to blame. "Well at least I'm not gay!" The same words might as easily have slipped out of Adam's or Eve's mouth as mine.

One of the great problems with Christians who feel shame is the comparisons that undoubtedly result. We often find a way to compare ourselves with someone who is not doing as good a job on the sin side of things as we think that we are. If we are trapped in pornography . . . at least we are not having premarital sex. And if we are having premarital sex . . . at least we are not homosexual. Even further, if we are engaging in homosexual acts . . . at least we are not into bestiality, child trafficking, or worse. It does not matter what our problem is, we will always be able to find someone else who is doing a "worse" job than we are at something else, so that we can feel better about ourselves. Call it "relative righteousness," but in the end it is all sin.

For some Christians, homosexuality has become the sin that people can point their finger at and find no fingers pointing back. With this form of blaming there is no understanding of the truth that we are all unworthy of being in relationship with God unless Christ intervenes. There is only the idea that some sins are better than others, and that the people who commit the worse sins are worse people. And furthermore, that God is judging us all based on who is the worst. This is what I had initially done when my friend told me of her struggle with her sexual orientation. I had compared, and I had blamed. In my mind, I had taken the focus off of myself; but the honest truth was, it did not make me feel any better.

Individual Reflection / Group Discussion

Have there been times in your life when you have pointed out others' sins in an effort to take the focus off of yourself?

Have you ever felt like the person who is being judged by everyone else? What did that feel like? If not, what might that feel like?

8

HONEST COMMUNITY

I remember being in college and having an organization called XXX Church[1] come and share with the campus. The guys had a get-together in the morning called "Porn and Pancakes," so I went, wondering what it was all about. A guy shared, and all of the students in the building were moved—I am sure—to fight against the temptation of pornography. But there was one problem—we were all lying to each other, and we did not even know it.

Here is how this all played out: One of the college campus leaders asked us to break off into small groups and share with each other the first time we had ever viewed porn, the last time we had ever viewed porn, and then talk about what types of things we like to do in order to avoid viewing porn when tempted. I was amazed at how my group of nine guys started sharing. However, I was definitely not amazed in a good way.

The first guy, one of the spiritual student leaders on campus, shared and said that he liked to keep his door open when he was on his computer so that he would be less tempted to look at pornography in his dorm. He always dressed nice and spoke in a way that told everyone he was in tune with God. Everyone nodded their heads in agreement as he told of his remedy for pornography. A second guy, feeding off of guy number one, said that he constantly had worship music playing in his room, even when he was gone, so that his space was always being consecrated to God. Both of these young men were respected on campus as leaders, so it was natural that they share first. They both spoke boldly and everyone listened. This set the stage for the kind of sharing that would take place for the beginning of the meeting. Neither of the two *leaders* answered the first two questions that had been asked, and as a result, no one was being transparent. This type of masquerading went on for about fifteen minutes while the guys who talked seemed to feel better about themselves, and the guys who did not only sat in silence. I looked over at a friend of mine who was in the same small group. I rolled my eyes at him—there was a lot of sewing and hiding happening in the room. We were all avoiding honest conversation; and although I was borderline terrified, I finally decided to speak.

I started off by saying that the first time I looked at porn was when I was little, giving a descriptive account of "the woman in the red dress on television." And then I discussed the last time I looked at porn . . . which was approximately two weeks before. I mentioned that I had gone into the campus computer lab by myself. I thought that I was going to be okay, but eventually I ended up clicking around and viewing pornography. The entire group fell silent. I had been the first to come out from behind my hiding place and reveal that my fig leaves were not really working. I was naked before an audience of other sewers and hiders, and I had no idea what was about to happen, but I can say confidently that I was afraid.

I was afraid of people telling me that I was screwed up. That there was no way I was going to get my life together unless I conformed to some sort of step-by-step process to rid myself of the sin. However, I was tired of thinking of myself as utterly disgusting and messed up, so I had taken a shot at the possibility that someone else in the group might stand up and be honest too. It happened. To my surprise, shock, and disbelief, it happened. The first guy who shared said that he had looked at porn a week ago, and then five minutes later (after additional guys became vulnerable and had shared openly), changed his story to four days ago.

I was feeling greatly encouraged by this level of honesty, and then a friend of mine in the group started sobbing. He said that he had looked at porn the night before, knowing that he was going to attend "Porn and Pancakes" the next morning. "Today," he said, "I feel dirtier than ever." In my mind I wondered if other guys in the group were saying to themselves, "At least I'm not as bad as that guy"; and then I realized that something much more beautiful was happening in that moment. Guys were dropping their fig leaves, coming out of hiding, and instead of blaming each other or comparing sins, men were being honest with each other. In that moment, I felt like I was standing before God. Everyone was uncovered. Everyone was laid bare. Because of grace, everyone was okay; and no matter what anyone struggled with in their life, honesty was the most powerful weapon we had. Our fellowship brought freedom.

I understand that my choice to become vulnerable and transparent with a group of men who were not was a risk. A huge risk. There was great potential for me to have been burned at the proverbial stake. All of my fears might have been met in the exact ways I was hoping they would not. The entire group might have told me I was screwed up, and rejected me. And I am sure this scenario has literally happened to others who have taken a risk similar to mine.

I heard the story of a woman who was actually fired from a church after seeking help for a common personal struggle. The woman was open and transparent, and instead of being received with grace and helped through a process of healing, she was rejected. However, the rejection was not her fault; and for her, healing was more important than saving face.

People who reach this level of transparency and remain consistent in it usually do find immense amounts of healing. In many ways, this is why we all fear transparency at times. We do not want to be rejected because we know we have all rejected others at times. But for those of us who can push through this fear toward authenticity, we eventually find a transformative grace that does not leave us hanging. Instead we find ourselves continually moving toward healing.

Despite my powerful and freeing experience with the group of men, I still have the tendency to make statements such as, "At least I'm not . . ." But I know that one day I will be caught in a place where I am at a completely equal level of dependence on God as those whom I have raised myself above. I think that the moment I stand before God for the first time will be the most humbling experience of my eternal life. Paul alludes to this idea in I Corinthians when he writes:

> By the grace God has given me, I laid a founda-
> tion as a wise builder, and someone else is build-
> ing on it. But each one should build with care. For
> no one can lay any foundation other than the one
> already laid, which is Jesus Christ. If anyone builds
> on this foundation using gold, silver, costly stones,

wood, hay or straw, their work will be shown for what it is, because the Day will bring it to light. It will be revealed with fire, and the fire will test the quality of each person's work. If what has been built survives, the builder will receive a reward. If it is burned up, the builder will suffer loss but yet will be saved—even though only as one escaping through the flames.[2]

While I know that moment will be humbling, I am learning that the best way to bring the gospel of Jesus to this world is to be broken and humbled *now*, before both God and people.

Individual Reflection / Group Discussion

Have you ever taken a risk and been transparent with a person or a group of people? Were you burned or received with grace? What was the experience like?

Have you ever had someone open up to you? Did you respond judgmentally or graciously? What was that experience like?

9

HONESTY IS THE POINT

I was talking with a friend of mine a little while ago, and he brought up the idea that at some point we need to move past honesty and begin being productive with our lives by overcoming sin. He said that if we view authenticity as the end result of a lifestyle, then we could ultimately use honesty to give ourselves permission to sin. Although I can see where my friend may have a point, I also see a huge danger in this way of thinking. Christianity is not about self-improvement. Christianity is about Jesus and what He has done for us.

Trying to get past honesty and to stop sinning can have the same end result as living in secret in regard to sin. When we are living in secret, there is a good chance we are trying to overcome sin by ourselves. We do this so that we can someday enter, perfectly and cleanly, into "honest" relationships . . . relationships where we will not have to reveal any individual weaknesses because we will have already overcome them. In the same way, if our honesty is only a temporary "fix" until we can actually conquer our sin, the ultimate focus is still on ourselves and our performance rather than on authentic relationship. Let me be clear: honesty is not something to move past; it is a lifestyle that we choose to live, living in the light as He is in the light, in order to have fellowship.

One of the arguments I hear in regard to the ultimate goal of over-coming sin is taken from Romans 6:1–2 where Paul writes, "What shall we say, then? Shall we go on sinning so that grace may increase? By no means! We are those who have died to sin; how can we live in it any longer?" Although what Paul is saying here is true—that we need not use the grace of God as an *excuse* to sin—reading those verses alone and not continuing to Romans 7 is a dangerous idea, simply because of what follows!

In Romans 7:15 Paul writes, "I do not understand what I do. For what I want to do I do not do, but what I hate to do." In a moment of honesty—and although he has previously written to the Romans that the grace of God is not an excuse to sin—Paul writes that he still continues to sin in ways that he wishes he would not. I find this amazing, because we do not see many in Christian circles being honest like this today. Instead we hear arguments on how we need to move past *simply being honest* and figure out how to quit sinning.

Ultimately, I feel that our greatest struggle is not to overcome sin—Jesus did that when He died for us on the cross and rose from the dead. Our greatest struggle is learning to live honestly with each other, and then it is acknowledging the victory accomplished by Jesus in His death and resurrection. And when we are trying so hard to overcome sin on our own, or spending all of our time asking God to take it away, we in turn are allowing the fear of being open before community to put us in a place where we think we need to be per-fect—or at least not as bad as others—before we can be seen fully. During these times we may use honesty as a tool to absolve our-selves from our own responsibility, and this is not honesty. This is hiding and blaming. As I said before, we cannot stop at being honest once or twice, or when we feel it's convenient. Honesty is a lifestyle.

Individual Reflection / Group Discussion

Do you agree with the statement that we need to "move past honesty"? Why or why not?

Consider Paul's words in Romans 7, specifically verse 15. How does his transparency in this chapter make you feel?

10

FELLOWSHIP EQUALS FREEDOM

A great moment of healing for me came when I decided to seek the Lord with a fast regarding my struggle with pornography. I knew I needed healing from the wounds created by negative sexual struggles and experiences in my life, and my goal was to pursue God's healing. During the fast Anna and I decided to visit her parents for the weekend. I was nervous that one of them might ask why I was fasting, and I tried to prepare myself for every question and scenario before we arrived at their house. The conversation didn't come up for most of the weekend, until one afternoon during a drive with Anna's father. We were alone, and I felt a bit nervous about having the conversation—not because I thought I would use manipulative language to protect myself from being fully seen, but because I had no idea how my wife's father would respond to his son-in-law's struggle with pornography.

We made small talk in the truck, and then he asked the question: "So, what are you fasting about?" I decided at that point to let it all out. I explained that I had been having a difficult time when I got a computer and that I was really trying to get a grip on things. Instead of shooting me with his double-barreled shotgun and telling me to get away from his daughter, he lifted me up with grace and encouraged me. I cannot emphasize enough how wonderful this made me feel. The conversation was quite similar to those I had shared with accountability partners, but it drew more authority coming from my wife's dad. In more words than I am using now, he told me to not be so hard on myself—referring to guilt and shame—and that he would lift me up in prayer. The fellowship that resulted with my father-in-law because of this conversation was simply grace. I had chosen to be honest, and God showed up—with a grace much bigger than I could have ever thought.

Even now looking back on this conversation, I see an entry point into the amazing freedom that was waiting for me. In that moment not only did I experience a fellowship that equaled freedom, but my transparency introduced me to a transformative grace . . . a grace so miraculous that pornography lost authority over my life. Simply, pornography was put under my feet; and bringing its ugliness before my father-in-law was a benchmark moment in that process, setting the stage for genuine transformation in my life.

Before talking with my wife's father, I had been living honestly with my wife, accountability partners, and even my own father about my struggle with pornography. However, this moment with my father-in-law had set the stage for something greater. After that conversation a ceiling was lifted. In a much greater way it allowed me to be shamelessly honest with more people who would pray and spiritually fight for my freedom from oppression. Another way of saying this: I quit managing what people knew about me and what they did not. I became ruthlessly honest. I became honest with people I knew could help me. As this circle of people who desired to fight for me became larger and more intentional (including the prayers of my own father and counseling) the authority that pornography held over me was removed. Honesty opened the door to a greater freedom than I could have ever imagined.

This did not occur because of my working harder. Again, Christianity is not about self-improvement. My freedom came about because grace transforms and does not leave us in the same place forever. Honesty moves us into grace, grace moves us into fellowship, and fellowship moves us into definitions of freedom that we did not even know existed. True fellowship allows others to fight for us with prayers, love, grace, and a hope that does not disappoint. And that equals freedom.

Paul writes in the book of Galatians, "It is for freedom that Christ has set us free."[1] Saying this is like saying, "It is for incredible taste that we eat delicious food." God desires to set us free from the power of darkness, which hides in secrecy. He wants us to see that we have the choice to be in an intimate, vulnerable, and honest relationship with Him. This is opposed to living in a realm of secrets where we feel as though we are the *only one* who has a particular struggle.[2] In one grace-filled conversation—one moment of knowing that I was not alone—one moment of true honesty, of "walking in the light,"[3] I experienced more grace than I might have ever known.

This was fellowship, and this fellowship was freedom. Freedom did not come from striving to live a perfect life or somehow becoming successful in overcoming my shortcomings on my own. Freedom came as a result of being immersed into relationships where I did not have to fix myself before I could live in community. This community was a place where I could let a thousand secrets out of my unseen closet and knew that my heart would be handled with care.

Because of that, my wounds could heal. And it all began with honesty. But the end result was not about not sinning. Being authentic created an outcome where I was placed under a blanket of grace so big that it made me never want to keep another secret again, simply because I did not have to live like that anymore. I was now living a lifestyle that matched what Paul said in Romans when he wrote,

> Do not conform to the pattern of this world, but be transformed by the renewing of your mind. Then you will be able to test and approve what God's will is—his good, pleasing and perfect will.[4]

When we know that it is okay to be vulnerable with another member of Christ's body, then we know that it is okay to stand naked before the Creator of our universe.

I understand that my father-in-law could have responded to me with disgust and judgment. He could have told me I was the worst person in the world and that I did not deserve his daughter. And to be honest, I feel a great deal of empathy for anyone who has had that kind of experience . . . where they have been judged and condemned after being transparent. But it's not worth giving up. For some of us, going through the pain of rejection in order to find true fellowship needs to become worth it. The truth is that learning to live in the light will ultimately bring fellowship, and this fellowship will open up doors to a greater freedom in one's life. Hiding and isolating out of fear or past hurts will never lead us to healing and grace. And ultimately, healing and grace are exactly what we need.

Individual Reflection / Group Discussion

I have proposed the idea that true fellowship equals freedom. Do you agree with this idea? Why or why not?

What are some ways you have experienced greater freedom through fellowship?

Part 2

THOUGHTS ON HONESTY AND THE CHURCH

11

VISITING CHURCH

When I was in the sixth grade my family moved to Dodge City, Kansas. My dad found a job at a local hospital in the town. Upon our arrival we began searching for a church that would best fit our family's needs, one that understood Jesus and the Bible in a way that would help my sister and me grow up in the most mature possible Christian environment.

On one occasion I remember going to church near one of the major highways in the city. The service was vibrant and exciting as we walked into the song-filled sanctuary. The preacher gave a passionate sermon about the gospel. There were many "amens" throughout and everyone was excited and thankful to have been to church that morning. Once the sermon was finished and the final song began—right as I thought we were about to leave—the strangest thing happened. The preacher stood up, said that Jesus had come down and stood right in front of him, and told him that someone had an issue with an eye. This, at first, made me feel awkward; but I rolled with the idea that Jesus might have come down from heaven and stood before this man. (I assumed he was speaking more figuratively anyway.) A woman then came up crying because she had been poked in the eye with a pine needle earlier that week. To which the preacher said that she was going to be healed.

This type of activity went on for quite some time, the preacher calling more people forward and telling more people they would be healed. There was a sort of encouraging feeling in the room as people appeared to be affected by healing power; and although I still felt somewhat awkward, I was beginning to look for positive elements within the service. Then the preacher made an extremely outlandish claim. He said, "If anyone in here is sick today, you either have no faith or you are living in sin!" At that moment my dad leaned over to my mom and whispered, "I do not think we should tell them that I work in a hospital." We never went back to that church again.

More than what the "sick" in that service encountered, I wonder what happened to the preacher the next time he got the flu. Even more, I wonder what caused the preacher to have this particular conviction. Maybe he had once been sick and at the same time been hiding sin in his life. God might have brought this truth to his attention, so the preacher began telling others that if they were sick, it was because they were also hiding sin. I do not know if this was actually the case, but for one reason or another, this guy had God's power worked out into a formula, and he was telling others that if they did not conform to his teaching, they were going to end up sick in bed.

Sometimes we have the tendency, when we experience God in one way, to immediately tell others that the way in which we experience Him is the only way. We expect others to obey in the same way, in order for them to experience God in any way. This is a scary thought, yet I know that messages like this are preached in churches all across our world. I have heard them.

There is a story in 2 Kings 6:1–7 where Elisha, by the power of God, makes an ax head, which had fallen into a body of water, float. It is one thing for everyone to be in awe of God's power after an instance such as that, and it is another thing for Elisha to walk around the circle of men who were there and tell them all to do the same thing in order to prove that they were operating under God's anointing.

Perhaps a similar event happened to this preacher in Kansas. And by creating this prescription for accessing God's healing power, this pastor was preventing members of his congregation from living in honesty together. No one wants to be honest about sickness or weakness in their life if they know that, in their honesty, someone else is going to tell them that there is ultimately something wrong with them. This is shaming. I find it hard to believe that anyone in that church community would want to open up and be vulnerable in any way. Even my dad did not want anyone to know where he worked.

More than the realization that honesty would not be received with grace was the underlying possibility of a deeper motivation for this kind of theology. Maybe one of the reasons this particular preacher was telling people that they needed to not sin—or to have more faith in order to stay healthy—was because this shifted the focus from him to the sin of others. This seems a lot like the blaming that happened in the garden of Eden.

One of the reasons I believe we always think we have to shift the focus off of ourselves in churches and onto other "sinners" is we do not believe that if we are open and honest with each other—and God—there will be enough grace for everyone. For example, if a preacher sat at the dinner table with his family "bad-mouthing" one of the members of his congregation on the night before a Sunday morning sermon, he might undoubtedly feel guilt. This might motivate a strong urge to preach against gossip, in order to subconsciously make himself feel and appear as though he is an *overcomer* of sin. However, if this man were to be honest with himself and others around him, he would more than likely find that there were others in his circle struggling with the exact same issue. Again, honesty brings fellowship, and grace-filled fellowship brings freedom.

I believe this is why James 5:16 says, "Therefore confess your sins to each other and pray for each other so that you may be healed. The prayer of a righteous person is powerful and effective." Obviously the righteous men James is speaking of here also sin like everyone else; the only difference is they are honest with themselves and others.

Proverbs 24:16 says, "For though the righteous fall seven times, they rise again, but the wicked stumble when calamity strikes." Getting back up involves grace, and grace involves honesty. Remember, Jesus did not come for the healthy (Mark 2:17) even if "healthy" means fakers. Jesus came for those who desire to push themselves to live in the light (honesty) and acknowledge that they cannot get there unless they are rescued from the secrets of darkness living.

What if the church could be the same to people today as Jesus was during his time spent on this earth? We know that when Jesus came, he confronted those who pretended to be spiritually adept, making the notion clear that only God was holy, and brought grace to those who were ready to acknowledge their position before Him as flawed and in desperate need of His touch.

I love the story in John 8, when Jesus confronts those who think of themselves as better and more spiritual than others. The Pharisees want to stone a woman caught in adultery and Jesus stops them in their tracks. His famous quote from John 8:7 still hits me every time I read it: "Let any one of you who is without sin be the first to throw a stone at her." There really is no room to blame anyone when we are all guilty. There is also no need to hide when we are in a true community. Finally, there is much less of a desire to make ourselves appear spiritual and clean when everyone can see our flaws.

I believe there comes a time in every church when we agree, as individuals and communities, that we are either going to preach a gospel of performance-based living—of "not sinning"—or a message of grace and acceptance, no matter what, and with no ifs, ands, or buts. Ultimately, this decision sets the stage for whether or not our members will walk in the light by living honestly with each other.

The greatest realization of this epiphany came to me when I was in high school and attending a statewide midyear Christian retreat over Christmas break with my youth group. The speaker, at what was called "In Depth," had given a typical sermon as to how we were supposed to live, and that if we felt like we needed to rededicate our lives to Jesus we should do that. He also mentioned that if there was something not right in our lives, like a sin we needed to confess or whatnot, we might want to come forward to the altar and meet with a counselor who would then take us to another room to talk and pray.

I suppose that none of this message was bad or wrong, but for one reason or another I was under the impression that if I went forward to pray I would somehow magically be made better and struggle less with sin. Of course I made my way to the front of the auditorium like I had almost a billion times before at other retreats and services, and I waited for the person who would tell me that God wanted me to give all of my life to Him and then pray with me that I would have enough strength to say no to the Devil and live a life of holiness. This is how the altar scenario normally went down at church retreats.

However, what was surprising and revelatory about this particular experience is the actual person who came to meet me at the altar. There was an assembly line of leaders who stood near the side wall while teenagers came forward; then a leader and a youth would walk to the back toward the meeting room in pairs. I must have gotten a good pick. The young man who I was given to talk with listened closely as I told him my circumstance, and how I desperately wanted to make God number one in my life. Usually at this point the person I was talking with would say, "Let me pray for you," and we would both, shortly after, be sent on our way (after I had filled out a card that said I had rededicated my life to Jesus). But this young man did something totally different that has stuck with me for a long time. He simply looked into my eyes and said some of the most profound words to ever be uttered by a Kansas high school Baptist youth leader in the history of the world. He said, "Me too, I struggle with the same thing. Let's pray for each other." All of a sudden—in the middle of Topeka, Kansas—I was brought to a place where the grace of Jesus Christ and humanity collide. I was brought to a place where two people were being openly honest with each other. No one was telling the other how each needed to live or what they needed to do in order to stop sinning. We were simply being together, being vulnerable, and being okay.

I realized in that moment that a student and a teacher can be on the same page in the kingdom of grace. A prostitute and a Pharisee can be brought to the same level when honesty and grace run into and over the other. A beautiful formation of something glorious occurs, like when the sky and those who can see only its vastness experience the momentum of its wonder in the wind, when community is understood enough for one human being to say to another, "Me too, I struggle with the same thing. Let's pray for each other."

When I envision a church that has made the decision to teach a message of grace, as opposed to a performance-based doctrine of not sinning, I see a place where people are treated like I was treated at the youth retreat. Honestly, I do not remember the man's name who prayed with me that day, but I know that I will see him again in heaven; and when I do, I will thank him for giving me a vision of how the church of God can present grace to a world that stands for individual achievement and religious success.

Individual Reflection / Group Discussion

Have you ever had an experience in a church community where you felt like you could or could not be honest? What happened?

Can you think of a time when you wished someone else would confess something to you so that you could say "Me too"?

12

THE CHURCH AND HOMOSEXUALITY

Throughout history, whether in creeds, doctrines, or church bulletins, people have always seemed to rally around what they believe. We can see this in people groups from the beginning of time. In history, the Mesopotamians served different gods, offered sacrifices to these different gods, and raised their children to believe in these gods too. I would imagine that if the Mesopotamians ever happened to run across another people group who believed something different than they, there might have been some type of a problem.

Even later, as humans progressed through the landscape of time, people killed each other for not believing the same things. I once heard that John Calvin burned a man at the stake for refusing to accept some of his specific beliefs.[1] To me all of this seems rather odd, especially when I consider phenomena such as the Crusades and other genocides; but for some reason or another our church today considers similar kinds of actions acceptable. Even though such actions do not involve actual physical killing, when it comes to people who think differently than we do, the church is ready to attack. Specifically, homosexuals[2] and those questioning their sexuality have, in this way, been humiliated and ostracized by the church at large for far too long.

It is important to know that when we talk about honesty, we are talking about more than simply sexual sin. Sexual sin is a sin that is often hidden by individuals, and so when talking about secrets, it is many times a common thread for a majority of people. However, there are plenty of other aspects of people's lives that need to be brought into the open. Idolatry, thievery, greed, slander, selfishness, lying, envy, gossip, and the like are all examples, and they are just a few of what might be listed.[3] I have specifically chosen to talk about homosexuality in this chapter because it is a hot topic among churches, and I feel some light needs to be shed on some of the ideas being passed around today.

Historically the Christian church, both Catholic[4] and many Protestant,[5] have taken the stance that homosexuality is not God's will for human beings. However, the paradigm has begun to shift in mainline and less conservative denominations with a handful of these churches teaching that homosexuality is not a sin.[6] This seems to have led to multiple stances on the topic with many political opinions. However, when a person's identity is tied up in their sexual orientation, sometimes opinions can be the most hurtful.

I have a friend who on two separate occasions was kicked out of her church community. The first time she was asked to leave (after going to her youth leader in vulnerability and confidence) because she simply thought she might be homosexual and was struggling with how she might identify herself. The second church she attended, and where she began once again building relationships, asked her to leave because she was beginning to believe that she was, in fact, homosexual. I heard this story while we were eating dinner together, and in an instant found myself apologizing on behalf of the entire church, historically and today, for wounding one of

God's children in such a way by telling her that she did not belong to His body.

A few years later I found this same friend of mine in a church located in a completely different part of our nation, and she seemed comfortable and edified. I began to wonder how many different churches some people have to try before they either find a compassionate place or quit trying and become bitter from all the rejection. I realize now that this is a direct result of churches rallying around beliefs rather than people. The attitude in my friend's first church—that communicated a form of sin hierarchy—left her particular sin on the bottom so that even when she became honest she was condemned. This attitude created a culture of secrecy, which was not the gospel.

Many times churches even use Scripture to support their casting out of others. For instance, my friend was kicked out of church because in all of her honesty about her sexual orientation she could not complete a certain artificial checklist required to have fellowship with the rest of her church. I remember sitting in many different churches during my stages of growing up and hearing people discuss what might need to happen if a gay couple were to attend our church. This may not happen at every church, but I consider it enlightening to have heard these conversations. Usually at first everyone was sort of silent and then one by one stones began to fly at the invisible gay people standing in the front of the room. Someone would say that we are called to love everyone and so we need to accept these people. That idea was quickly shot down by a, "No! We need to love the sinner, but we cannot condone their sin." Usually at this point the first person would stand up and say that all sins are equal and that we all are in need of the same grace as everyone else. But eventually, no matter what was said during the time of discussion (that always ended in the same place—nowhere), someone would stand up and say, "Well what does the Bible say about this topic?" Bible passages have often been used to justify kicking homosexuals out of church.

Undoubtedly, the first chapter of Romans would be one of the first discussed. It is a passage many people use not only to prove *why* they believe homosexuality is wrong, but also to cast out homosexual people who have possibly never even been to their church (and if they have, probably will never return because of the negative response). It goes like this:

> The wrath of God is being revealed from heaven against all the godlessness and wickedness of people, who suppress the truth by their wickedness, since what may be known about God is plain to them, because God has made it plain to them. For since the creation of the world God's invisible qualities—his eternal power and divine nature—have been clearly seen, being understood from what has been made, so that people are without excuse.
>
> For although they knew God, they neither glorified him as God nor gave thanks to him, but their thinking became futile and their foolish hearts were darkened. Although they claimed to be wise, they became fools and exchanged the glory of the immortal God for images made to look like a mortal human being and birds and animals and reptiles.

> Therefore God gave them over in the sinful desires
> of their hearts to sexual impurity for the degrading
> of their bodies with one another. They exchanged
> the truth about God for a lie, and worshiped and
> served created things rather than the Creator—
> who is forever praised. Amen.
>
> Because of this, God gave them over to shameful
> lusts. Even their women exchanged natural sexual
> relations for unnatural ones. In the same way the
> men also abandoned natural relations with women
> and were inflamed with lust for one another. Men
> committed shameful acts with other men, and re-
> ceived in themselves the due penalty for their error.[7]

The trickiness of this chapter—and the entire book of Romans for
that matter—is not in what the apostle Paul wrote. The confusion
lies in how many in our church interpret this passage today. On
the surface one might say the meaning is obvious, that Paul wrote
Romans 1 in order to prove that acts such as men having sexual
intercourse with other men are wrong, and that we need to kick
people out of church if they have somehow begun a process where
they might eventually follow these perversions. However, this is not
what Paul is doing at all in the writing of the book of Romans.

Simply, Paul begins with Romans 1 in order to engage the readers
of this passage by showing them the sins of others who have no
excuse for turning away from God. Then Paul writes quite quickly in
the beginning of chapter 2 that those people who are condemning
and judging those mentioned in chapter 1 are also without excuse
because in whatever way, whether it be figurative or literal, they

are doing the exact same things! Romans 2:1 says, "You, therefore, have no excuse, you who pass judgment on someone else, for at whatever point you judge another, you are condemning yourself, because you who pass judgment do the same things." In a lot of cases, because of a misreading of Romans 1, homosexuality has become the sin that many Christians can point their finger at while no fingers point back at them. This is blaming.

Romans 3–6 follows with an excellent explanation of how all should live with an understanding of our humanness, and at the same time learn to stand up under the grace of Christ as we live lives worthy of the calling we have received (Ephesians 4:4). Romans 7 says that living a holy and righteous life on our own is physically and virtually impossible, but Romans 8 lets us know that because of Christ there is no condemnation over our heads, minds, or hearts. To me it sounds a lot like Paul is asking the church to quit blaming and condemning others and learn to give and receive God's grace through Jesus. Romans 9–11 explains how all the non-Jewish people, among whom homosexuality was to say the least not unknown, are invited into this redemptive grace. The rest of the book challenges and encourages God's people to love one another and get along in the church so God's mission can get done in telling and living out the good news about Jesus everywhere people are.[8] All of that to say, if we want to interpret Romans 1 as spiritual instruction for expelling homosexuals from our churches, then we also need to read Romans 2 and kick ourselves out right alongside the ones we are tagging as reprobate. We have fallen for Paul's plan in the same way the Romans did back then, and because of that we have become Pharisees ourselves. We are also without excuse. Maybe we need to think twice before we go kicking people out of church.[9]

I have heard Matthew 18:15–17 used in the same way as the above passage:

> If your brother or sister sins, go and point out their fault, just between the two of you. If they listen to you, you have won them over. But if they will not listen, take one or two others along, so that "every matter may be established by the testimony of two or three witnesses." If they still refuse to listen, tell it to the church; and if they refuse to listen even to the church, treat them as you would a pagan or a tax collector.

In order to use Matthew 18 as a tool for confronting someone in regard to any form of sin, the situation must be identified as a personal offense. This does not specifically point to homosexuality. Furthermore, sexual immorality is sin against one's *own* body.[10]

As the church we are either going to be grace to people or we are going to demand that others conform to a list of rules and regulations. As far as treating someone as I would treat a tax collector (someone who sinned for a living), I refer to Jesus' actions in Luke 19:1–10:

> Jesus entered Jericho and was passing through. A man was there by the name of Zacchaeus; he was a chief tax collector and was wealthy. He wanted to see who Jesus was, but because he was short he could not see over the crowd. So he ran ahead and climbed a sycamore-fig tree to see him, since Jesus was coming that way.

When Jesus reached the spot, he looked up and said to him, "Zacchaeus, come down immediately. I must stay at your house today." So he came down at once and welcomed him gladly.

All the people saw this and began to mutter, "He has gone to be the guest of a sinner."

But Zacchaeus stood up and said to the Lord, "Look, Lord! Here and now I give half of my possessions to the poor, and if I have cheated anybody out of anything, I will pay back four times the amount."

Jesus said to him, "Today salvation has come to this house, because this man, too, is a son of Abraham. For the Son of Man came to seek and to save the lost."

Now we know how Jesus responds to sinners. After all, this is the same way He responds to us. Maybe we can try to be like Him. (It is also interesting to note that the writer of Matthew 18 was in fact a tax collector himself!)

The issue with the church and homosexuality is not whether homosexuality is right or wrong. The issue is whether or not we will receive the homosexual in the same way that Christ has received us.

The church has not been a safe place for all people, and because of that we are not an honest community. I am attempting to dilute this controversy in order to bring to light this truth: we are called to love all people in the same way that Christ loves all people.

When we read and hear that God hates sin, we must know that this is not because God is a judgmental and spiteful God who would put us in situations that ultimately lead to His destruction of us. God hates sin because He loves us, and sin causes us to be unaware of how much He loves us. God does not hate sin because He wants to throw lightning bolts at us. He hates sin because sin hurts us.

One argument for why God hates sin is that He is perfect, holy, and righteous, and cannot tolerate sin. Like many, I learned this growing up in church and often felt like God hated me because I was not perfect, let alone holy or righteous. However, to know that God hates sin because He loves me (and sin skews my perception of this) does agree with the truth that God is perfect, holy, and righteous. It also allows me to know and embrace the truth that His perfection, holiness, and righteousness culminate in love. As we also learned in Sunday school: God is love.

Several years ago, a friend of mine called to ask me if I still thought he was going to hell. He was gay, and for several years before this phone conversation, I had attempted to "fix" him through proving that not only was homosexuality wrong, it was a choice, and that he needed to not have this struggle. I never thought that he was going to hell, and I never told him that he was. But somewhere along the line, he received that message from me. It wasn't my intention, and it wasn't my heart. My desire to be right had overwhelmed and drowned any outward expression of my unconditional love for my friend.

Some people may have never experienced something like I did in the story above; but we all can replace one sin, like homosexuality, with any number of other sins: materialism, gossip, lying, gluttony, judging, and so on, and the result can easily be the same. Our desire to "rescue" someone from their sin can be mistaken for judgment and thus overpower any expression of unconditional love.

So perhaps, even when we speak in love—even when we have the best intentions, even when we surround our exhortative words with the most gracious of speech—perhaps even then we are communicating the lies of otherness, rejection, and unacceptance. Even then, with our best intentions, we may fail to communicate the truth of the gospel of Jesus Christ, which exclaims God's reality that all are loved, all are welcome, all are desired, and all are accepted. This, His gospel, is an honest grace.

Again, homosexuality has become the lifestyle to which Christians can point their fingers without any pointing back. No matter what our struggle, we always look for someone *worse* than we are so that we can feel better about ourselves. This is not only wrong, it is ridiculous. The attitude in church that communicates any form of ranking of sins will always leave one sin on the bottom. This can only lead to a culture of secrecy. And where there is secrecy there is no grace. If the church cannot get over the ideas of political rightness and wrongness in regard to how we respond to others' choices, then we will never be able to invite others into the grace of Jesus Christ.

Individual Reflection / Group Discussion

What are your thoughts on how the church has handled the issue of homosexuality?

How can the church better represent Christ in our response to the issue of homosexuality?

13

COMMUNAL HONESTY
AND INTIMACY

There was a moment in the garden of Eden when Adam and Eve first laid eyes on each other. What stands out to me the most is that both Adam and Eve were as physically vulnerable as possible, and neither of them felt ashamed or awkward. We read in the last verse of Genesis 2 that they were both unashamed, and so I can imagine they had an extremely high level of transparency, even to the point of physical intimacy. Adam and Eve knew each other in every way (emotional, spiritual, and physical).

Recently I have been thinking quite a bit about the idea of honesty and intimacy and have been wondering about the risk one must take in order to experience grace and gain true communal relationship with another. Basically, if someone wants to be loved for all that he is, he must first let another *know* all that he is.

I can imagine Adam running to Eve, completely unashamed, and saying, "Here I am baby! All of me. Take it or leave it." To which Eve replied, "This is all I know of you! I will definitely take all that I can get." Ultimately, there is a huge risk involved in being laid bare before someone else, flaws and all. It forces them to choose what they are going to do with who we have presented ourselves to be. However, this is a choice that must be made.

Once I was sitting outside with two friends discussing the issue of an individual's vulnerability and how it relates to Christian community. I remember making a comment that I believed honesty created intimacy. I was saying that vulnerability or "laid bareness," as the Bible talks about in Genesis, is a characteristic that is able to breed intimate "knowing." I thought I was on to some sort of epiphany. I felt that I had obtained an adequate knowledge of the Genesis account: I had studied the stories of the beginning of time, and I had also written a book that largely dealt with similar topics like the one I was bringing to my friends' attention. Simply, I felt that I was entering into a kind of teaching moment with my friends as they listened intently to what I was saying. However, within a few minutes of my sophisticated terminology, one of my friends interrupted by saying, "I don't necessarily agree," which got me listening. She said, "I think that honesty can breed intimacy only if the people receiving the honesty of another have spirits of humility." My friend was right. One cannot receive another's honesty graciously unless he first becomes a safe place himself—unless he is willing to accept anyone in the same way that Christ accepts him. Forgiveness is an all-inclusive, timeless lifestyle to be lived.

Many people in our culture are simply afraid of coming to church or even experiencing a relationship with someone who claims to know Jesus. This is often because claiming to know Jesus is many times synonymous with rallying around a doctrine that historically excludes far more individuals than it accepts. The idea of unabashedly revealing oneself to a community is almost a foreign concept in church today. This is largely because those in the church have not chosen to become honest first. What if the Christian church could be a place where everyone, followers of Christ and those who don't know Christ, felt safe enough to be vulnerable before their community, and knew that in doing so they would be accepted for who they were, and given the freedom to heal?

This kind of question is not one that can easily be answered. First, this question is abstract. Second, a question such as this one can only be answered through action. It is the same as saying, "What would happen if I drove this car as fast as it can go?" One will never know what might happen until the action is followed through, until the "what if" question is answered with action. To that explanation I ask again, what if the church could be a place where everyone felt safe enough to be weak before their community, and knew that in doing so they would be accepted? Could we truly express ourselves like Paul does in 2 Corinthians 12:10, "For when I am weak, then I am strong"?

This kind of commitment—to be a church that is open to all people—can be a difficult transition. And more than that, becoming vulnerable yourself first, and then setting this example in church for others to see, takes humility. It is opening oneself up to the potential of rejection, like asking a girl to dance. Yet many guys have gone ahead and asked the girl to dance anyway, knowing that the reward for asking might be far greater than the possibility of the girl saying no.

The reward for living honestly is greater than simply getting something off of one's chest. It is fellowship, grace, and many times a greater freedom than was known before transparency was embraced. This may be a stretch for some, but I do believe that churches can become places of honesty, communities "living in the light," so much so that people who are sick and tired of living in secret can open themselves up to a greater acceptance than they might have ever thought. Imagine a church that embraces honesty so well that it is known as a place of transformational grace. A church like this sounds a bit like heaven, or at least a place that prepares people for heaven. To me this kind of living embraces the gospel. Like Paul says in Romans (during one of his greatest moments of honesty and vulnerability), "There is now no condemnation for those who are in Christ Jesus."[1] We may all come to the cross together, naked and unashamed.

In order for this kind of intimacy to occur, there would definitely need to be a significant showing of honesty. Some may argue that the pulpit is not a confessional, that a preacher does not need to tell a congregation about his sin, and that it might be unhealthy. I guess I do not necessarily want to ask all preachers to let all of their secrets out when they get up to preach next Sunday, but I do want to ask that leaders of Christian churches begin to live lifestyles of honesty that give the people involved in their communities permission to also live lifestyles of honesty. Grace only comes with honesty. We will never experience grace-filled fellowship unless we first experience honest relationships. Then we will know true freedom, because true freedom comes from unconditional love.

Individual Reflection / Group Discussion

How is physical intimacy encouraged by transparency?

Is it true that we will never experience grace unless we first risk honesty? Why or why not?

14

ROADBLOCKS

One major roadblock that I see in some of our attempts to live life-styles of honesty within our communities is that we always want to find the easiest possible way to get to the finish line. I remember sitting in church when I was in college, listening to the preacher talk about grace, and thinking, "I get it. Grace covers all of my sin, but when is this guy going to start talking about how to overcome specific sins so that I do not need as much grace in some areas?"

With grace and honesty I am pursuing a lifestyle that will continue for the remainder of my life, and there is no finish line. I do not get to walk through my front door someday and finally get to be finished living in the light with my wife. She will always need me to be honest; she will always need me to have grace for her, and vice versa. If we are to have a healthy marriage, we need to continually develop lifestyles of honesty with each other so that neither of us winds up keeping some secret that interferes with our fellowship. The only finish line is heaven, and God is going to take us there. We do not get to climb a ladder on our own.

For some reason or another, though, many Christians do still desire to get to the finish line before heaven, and we try to manipulate our way there. I am just as guilty in this as anyone else, but the thought of what I am doing still haunts me nonetheless. Instead of living transparently and admitting, let's say, that selling everything I have and giving it to the poor is difficult, I spend an afternoon volunteering at the local homeless shelter. Instead of inviting someone from a broken family to join me for a meal, or admitting that this is even difficult, I give her a few dollars as I pass by her on the street. In doing so, I am not only taking shortcuts, but I am also refusing to live honestly with myself about the hurting people in this world whom Christ has called me to love. I am also trying to tell myself I am crossing the finish line of holy living, when in reality I am not even close.

A story in Mark 10 helps us understand this concept in a greater way:

> As Jesus started on his way, a man ran up to him and fell on his knees before him. "Good teacher," he asked, "what must I do to inherit eternal life?"

> "Why do you call me good?" Jesus answered. "No one is good—except God alone. You know the commandments: 'You shall not murder, you shall not commit adultery, you shall not steal, you shall not give false testimony, you shall not defraud, honor your father and mother.'"

> "Teacher," he declared, "all these I have kept since I was a boy."

> Jesus looked at him and loved him. "One thing you lack," he said. "Go, sell everything you have and give

> to the poor, and you will have treasure in heaven.
> Then come, follow me."
>
> At this the man's face fell. He went away sad,
> because he had great wealth.[1]

I wonder if, when Jesus told the rich young ruler to sell everything he had, give it to the poor, and follow Him, Jesus would have been okay had the young man dropped to his knees, been honest, and told Jesus the task was too difficult for his selfish heart. I think Jesus would have forgiven him or at least entered into a life-transforming relationship with the young man, like God did with Isaiah in the Old Testament:

> In the year that King Uzziah died, I saw the Lord,
> high and exalted, seated on a throne; and the train
> of his robe filled the temple. Above him were ser-
> aphim, each with six wings: With two wings they
> covered their faces, with two they covered their
> feet, and with two they were flying. And they were
> calling to one another:
>
> > "Holy, holy, holy is the LORD Almighty;
> > the whole earth is full of his glory."
>
> At the sound of their voices the doorposts and
> thresholds shook and the temple was filled with
> smoke.
>
> "Woe to me!" I cried. "I am ruined! For I am a
> man of unclean lips, and I live among a people of
> unclean lips, and my eyes have seen the King, the

Lord Almighty."

Then one of the seraphim flew to me with a live
coal in his hand, which he had taken with tongs
from the altar. With it he touched my mouth and
said, "See, this has touched your lips; your guilt is
taken away and your sin atoned for."

Then I heard the voice of the Lord saying, "Whom
shall I send? And who will go for us?"

And I said, "Here am I. Send me!"[2]

However, instead of being like Isaiah and living in honesty with God,
and then as a result entering into a transformational grace, I have
convinced myself that there is some kind of a finish line I can cross
without needing to rely on God's intervention. This is not honesty.
It is avoidance. My ability to be honest then becomes blocked by my
own selfish desires to see only myself become complete. This is not
living in the light, and the result will not be fellowship.

Jesus tells us in Matthew 7:13 to enter through the narrow gate, and
that few people even find this gate at all. He also tells us in Luke
13:24 to enter through the narrow door. I understand the salvation
principles tied to these statements, but I also believe that this kind
of language, which Jesus seems to use often throughout his time of
teaching in the Gospels, points to the idea that Christianity is not
an easy road. Rather, following Jesus is difficult. This is also a reason why the reward is so great. And that is why Jesus tells us we
are not alone. In John 16:33 Jesus tells his disciples, "I have told you
these things, so that in me you may have peace. In this world you

will have trouble. But take heart! I have overcome the world." We humble ourselves before God, telling Him that we cannot achieve an abundant life on our own. We ask Him to forgive us for trying other alternatives, and He gives us grace and mercy. This results in a salvation that is greater than anything, and ultimately this lands us in heaven with our Father.

I see a direct parallel between our relationship with God and with living a lifestyle of honesty within community. We humble ourselves before each other, acknowledging that we are not as perfect as we would like to appear. We place our hearts on the table for each other to see, and because God has received us with grace, we show grace to each other. Then our fellowship builds a community that truly represents the body of Christ, one that other people want when they see it, which is precisely God's grace being extended to one another. Of course this isn't easy. Why? Many times we are too proud to humble ourselves, even if it is before the people who love us the most.

Individual Reflection / Group Discussion

Have you ever thought, "Once I conquer this specific hurdle in my life, I will have arrived"? How did that thinking work out?

How might a Christian community, practically speaking, prioritize being an honest Christian community in order to better represent the body of Christ?

15

BEING A SAFE PLACE

Karl Marx has said, "Philosophers have only interpreted the world in various ways. The point, however, is to change it."[1] I like to take this statement and change it up a bit. I say, Christians have only interpreted the church in various ways. The point, however, is to change it.

There came a time in church history when Christians began to divide based on beliefs and ways to do ministry. In the midst of figuring out the way Jesus asked us to live, Christ's body of believers was separated and segregated all across the world. Sadly enough, this period in history was a time that many fondly remember as the Reformation.

In 1517, Martin Luther wrote and posted the Ninety-Five Theses, marking the beginning of the Reformation and the separation from traditional Catholicism. The Reformation was then amended by John Calvin around 1536 with the publication of certain key works marking the start of the Reformed denomination. In the early 1520s, the Anabaptist denomination began to surface. From 1525 on, Ulrich Zwingli, John Calvin, and Martin Luther had tens of thousands of Anabaptists killed for their

rejection of infant baptism. Later, under Menno Simons's leadership, the Mennonite denomination was founded and through the
influence of Jakob Ammann, the Amish denomination evolved. In
1534 King Henry VIII became the "supreme head" of the English
Church, which led to more splitting. Eventually we arrive at the
ministry of John Wesley, who started the Methodist denomination, and John Smyth who started the General Baptist denomination.[2] Believe it or not, the list goes on and on. There was
arguing, fighting, and in some cases even murder over specific
beliefs.

Historically, our Christian communities have made it so that only
those who agree with a particular community's way of thinking
would be made comfortable enough to worship God. The problem with this was that everyone else, Christian or not, noticed this
behavior and tagged the church as no different from the rest of
the world. What the church had created, in a sense, was a political struggle over right and wrong, spirituality and non-spirituality.
And those most in need of Christian community were left feeling
as though the church was not a safe place to be honest and receive
grace.

People picked the church that best fit their particular belief system,
and then adapted the rest of their individual beliefs. The result was
precisely pseudo- or almost-community. Individuals were never
quite able to experience the fullness and grace of Christ's body
because honesty was never valued, and the truth that grace follows
a vulnerability of the heart was never realized. I understand I am
making a blanket statement, but I also believe that it is happening
in churches today, all around the world.

So how can the church become a safe place for people to enter into true community? I can imagine that the answers to that question are quite diverse and, for some, extremely complicated. My point in asking the question is not to provide an answer. If I did that we might all end up back in the same place we were when the question was posed, fighting and dividing over what we think is right and wrong . . . and deciding who is more spiritual. Nevertheless, the church does need to become a safe place for people to come and learn about what God has done for them. By that I mean God sending His Son to die for us all. I do not necessarily even believe that this kind of knowledge needs to be attained through a church service. After all, the church is not a building. It is not even a building of people. The church is the people of God, and together we need to become a safe place.

I remember sitting in a service on a Wednesday night when the topic "being a safe place" arose, and people began discussing what that might look like. What was strange to me then, but what I find to be quite normal in churches today, is that the majority of the conversation was about timing and when exactly new people who came into our church should be told that they were living lifestyles of sin. For instance, what if someone was a homosexual, or an alcoholic? If they came to church three Sundays in a row, when was the right time to talk to them about their sin?

I remember someone saying something about how it is the Holy Spirit who convicts of sin; and it is not our job to cast people in and out of church, as if we were separating sheep and goats.[3] But that idea did not seem to go over too well in that particular service. For some reason, people wanted to know how they were supposed to treat others who were living in sin; and until we figured that out, no one was going to be satisfied.

I do believe there is an answer to that question, and I also believe it is rather simple. We need to treat people exactly how God, because of Jesus, treats us. He forgives us, and He brings us into fellowship with Him. We need to cover others with grace. We need to receive others' vulnerability with love. There is never a circumstance that is beyond God's grace. Never. If there is honesty mixed with the knowledge of what Jesus did for us,[4] then there will be fellowship. And true fellowship equals freedom.

The church does have a responsibility to teach about sin, but it is not in the way the church has been teaching about sin. To stand against specific sins with a political rightness is different than saying that we all miss the mark of holiness. Telling people they are wrong is different than allowing each other to be honest about our lives and then express the grace that Jesus gave to all of us on the cross. The apostle Paul gives us a great way to address sin when dealing with other people. He tells us to think differently about sin, to see ourselves as the ones who need grace the most instead of other people. He writes:

> Here is a trustworthy saying that deserves full acceptance: Christ Jesus came into the world to save sinners—of whom I am the worst. But for that very reason I was shown mercy so that in me, the worst of sinners, Christ Jesus might display his immense patience as an example for those who would believe in him and receive eternal life.[5]

At some point, the church began deciding what other people needed to do in order to receive our fellowship. We did not necessarily raise banners with lists of people who were and were not allowed in our communities, but we did begin to send messages that unless people thought like us, looked like us, or acted like us, then they were not ready to receive God's grace. We have all kinds of excuses for this way of thinking. However, the bigger question is: When does it become okay to exclude?

Think about the Reformation again. Martin Luther nailed his theses to the door of the church, and we remember this as a good thing. And in many ways, it was. However, out of this happening, the church divided, and people even started killing each other over their beliefs! So somewhere along the line of Martin Luther figuring out God's grace for himself, people began to make more rules about who could be accepted into the church and who could not. I am sure this was not his intended outcome; but it just goes to show that humans really do like to be right, even taking that desire into conversations about God's grace. It is almost as if we want to be the ones who decide who gets in and who has to wait outside.

The good news is, however, that when we are dealing with the idea of Jesus dying on the cross for all of our sins to make us right with God, we must also never forget that because of His death everyone is invited into salvation. And if everyone is invited into salvation, then we, as the church, need to receive people in the exact same way as Christ receives us. No prerequisites. We need to simply be a place where honesty can reign free and grace can be received. The church must become a safe place for people to be laid bare before each other and Christ. If this does not occur, then we will perpetuate an exclusive gospel that is really no gospel at all.

Individual Reflection / Group Discussion

How can the church become more of a safe place for people to be honest as opposed to fake?

What do you think is the church's responsibility in regard to teaching about sin?

16

WHY HONESTY MATTERS

So why does honesty matter in the big picture? And more than that, even if honesty does matter for the individual, why is it so important to have entire church communities embracing this lifestyle?

If an individual can be laid bare completely before another, and in turn receive grace, then the result is the fellowship as talked about in 1 John 1:7 (as we walk in the light). This fellowship frees us to get our eyes away from ourselves in the mirror to focus on others and how we might love and be loved by them in return.

Now let's transition this lifestyle of honesty into an entire community of people but with two different communities as opposed to two different people. Take the following scenario: let's say that all the members of a church begin to live in individual honesty with each other, and the result is fellowship and freedom as mentioned earlier, with a greater understanding of God's grace. A member of the church then notices how much excess money is being poured into a new building fund or a church upgrade, versus putting the money into a needy community nearby or across the ocean. This person now feels he can be honest with his community about this issue, because he knows he will be received with grace, even if people disagree. This member sees another's pain and responds to it through beginning an honest conversation with his community. In this scenario, the community sits down together and takes a look at how much might be accomplished elsewhere with their resources. The church decides to put a halt to their project and instead open itself up to a relationship with another community somewhere else in the world that might use these resources more effectively. Perhaps this church discovers that it has been using excessiveness as distraction for honesty and true community. That they have been "hiding" on a corporate scale. And now they are free to love others instead. The church discovers a grace in giving to others that allows them to be free from the love of money and the need to hide behind excess.[1]

Why might this church reach this particular conclusion? Simple. Because of the intimate fellowship that is being experienced and the freedom that it brings. Grace has caused an entire community to stop focusing solely on itself and instead enter into a conversation about a world that is hurting and in need of help more than the church needs another upgrade. Freedom, in this case, brings opportunities that otherwise would have never been seen. This freedom came from fellowship, and this fellowship came from living in the light.[2]

The question that comes to my mind from the above scenario deals with the abundance in which many church communities already live. Could living in communal excess be a form of corporate hiding? In other words, is all of our "stuff" getting in the way of truly carrying out the mission of Jesus, namely caring for others? It is no secret that in chasing after material possessions one will never reach the finish line. There will always be more things and better things to acquire and consume, and fulfillment will never be reached. This pursuit of things can easily distract us from seeing those who need our help, not to mention the fact that owning the most beautiful, excellent, up-to-date everything can ostracize those who have less and make them feel as if they are the losing party in a competition for wealth.

There is a temptation to argue this question defensively with comments such as, "In that case, we should only worship in a barn and not have any hymnals, instruments, or even pay a pastor." I am not asking anyone to swing from one extreme to the other. I am not even advocating for all churches to sell their fog machines, their instruments, or their colored lights, and give the money away. Nice things in and of themselves are not the problem. However, it is important to remain vigilant and not let ourselves get caught up in or distracted by the acquisition of excess. My hope is that churches can begin to be safe enough places so that people can enter into conversations like the one mentioned above without being cynical or feeling alone. The real issue is people and relationships. Does my excess hinder relationships? Does our excess hinder relationships? I am simply hoping we can be honest about our abundance of excess in safe places where we can have real conversations, and be willing to ask God if there is any way we can use what we have been given to help our hurting neighbors around the world. God may not be calling us to live in poverty, but He may be calling us as individuals and churches to give sacrificially and free ourselves from the need to keep excess for ourselves.

The end result might culminate in a wealthy church choosing not to live in selfish abundance but, rather, to spend their excess resources sponsoring an entire orphanage of children.[3] This does not happen without honesty and the freedom to have this kind of conversation.

What if we could all live like this? It does not matter if we are part of a big community or a small one. The idea of communal honesty changes the way that we, as the church, love the world. The gospel is about living our lives with people as our priority, and receiving them with grace in the same way Christ receives us.

Individual Reflection / Group Discussion

Do you agree that individuals and churches trying to fix themselves and appear better have sometimes blinded them to the outside world? Why or why not?

How do you think living transparently can help you better see and engage a hurting world?

17

WALKABOUT

One of the most powerful experiences that I can remember sharing with a group of people happened on a trip called Walkabout. Each year, before fall semester, Greenville College takes a large group of student leaders into the Smokey Mountains of Tennessee to spend around ten days hiking, building community, and growing together as Christian leaders. On a couple of different occasions I have been asked to lead a team, and I do so enthusiastically. I love the outdoors. I love being with people. And I love being outdoors with people, especially if we have a common purpose. The teams are usually divided into groups of six to eight students with two leaders. Numbers vary, but the purpose is always the same: build community, grow together in faith, and have an awesome experience. To me Walkabout is a high point of experiential learning.

On one occasion I was leading a team of students with a good friend of mine, Scott. Scott and I had known each other for a long time and we had decided that year, since we were hiking through the Smokey Mountains, that it might be a good idea to take our team on a journey through David's Songs of Ascent. Essentially, these songs are found in the book of Psalms and go from chapters 120 to 134. During these songs, David is on a journey to worship the Lord.

He is on a pilgrimage, and he is definitely traveling. We see early in Psalm 121 that there is going to be some rugged terrain— that David's journey is not going to be easy. He says in Psalm 121:1, "I lift up my eyes to the mountains—where does my help come from?"

Scott and I felt that these Psalms might be perfect for our team that year, and so we began going through them on each hike that we made together. I remember being on top of a mountain with everyone and reading Psalm 121 aloud. The team resonated with what David was writing in those moments. We all agreed that hiking up the side of a mountain is difficult. God definitely made mountains challenging.

Our packs weighed between thirty and forty pounds each, which added to the challenge, but our team seemed to always press on at an exciting pace. It was as if no one wanted to be seen as the weakest member of the team. We all trudged through the pain and kept the most grueling pace we could possibly endure.

This was all fine and good until one day we misread the map, and a seven-mile hike turned into a sixteen-mile excursion, which at some points began to feel more like a death march than it did a community-building camping trip. However, we pressed on. Our pace was fast. The light was fading, evening was approaching, and then the worst happened. One of the female members of our team, Erika, began to have an asthma attack. Luckily we caught it before anything horrible occurred, and we decided to sit down and rest.

After a few short minutes, we decided that we needed to keep moving. It was getting dark, and we did not want anyone to get hurt due to not being able to see where we were stepping. We started trailblazing, and only a few minutes later, Erika was having trouble breathing again.

I quickly decided that we needed to empty her backpack and begin distributing her weight amongst the team. To me, this was simply a practical idea that would help us get to our campground safely. We took everything Erika was carrying and started shoving it into our own bags. As we were doing this she started to cry, so we stopped what we were doing and sat in a circle on the trail.

My thoughts about myself in that moment began to haunt me. I had pushed a team of people to their physical limit, but I had done so in an incredibly harmful way. Everyone in that team, including myself, had pushed ourselves as far as we physically could, and this was for the purpose of keeping up with everyone else. No one wanted to be the weakest link. Everyone wanted to carry their own weight to prove that they were good enough to hike with the rest of the trailblazers. But the truth was that we were all broken; Erika was just the first to break completely. She had been the one who had her pack emptied because she was struggling to keep pace. And the worst part of it all was I was the leader. I was the one who had propelled us into such a performance-based escapade on the mountain.

Surprisingly, just as quickly as I had realized my failure, I was reminded of Psalm 133. This was one of David's final songs as he approached the place of worship. He had been hiking for an incredibly long time and as he approached his destination, he wrote this Psalm:

> How good and pleasant it is
>   when God's people live together in unity!

It is like precious oil poured on the head,
    running down on the beard,
running down on Aaron's beard,
    down on the collar of his robe.
It is as if the dew of Hermon
    were falling on Mount Zion.
For there the LORD bestows his blessing,
    even life forevermore.

As we were sitting there in the circle we had formed on the trail, Scott reached in his bag, pulled out a bottle filled with Crystal Light drink mix and some bread. He had decided that we needed to share a meal together, and I had decided that I wanted to read Psalm 133 to everyone.

I am pretty sure we all shared some tears together that night. We realized that our duty together was not to keep up a relentless pace, proving to each other that we were not weak. Instead, our responsibility was to receive each other with humility as Christ had received us all. We realized that grace was about lifting up each other's burdens, and that if we could live in honesty with each other, as opposed to striving to be the best, then we could open up a huge opportunity to extend grace.

That moment on the trail, when Erika's bag was being poured out to her team members, was not about Erika being weak. It was about our team being unified. It was about us being one body. It was about the truth that if one of us did not make it to our next campsite, then none of us were going to make it. We were one body. We became one person.

Obviously Erika looks back on that story and talks about how grace comes with honesty, and that she learned that she does not need to prove herself in Christian community. But what I learned during that hiking trip was that I can either drive people to make themselves acceptable before *me*, or I can be like Christ, lifting up each person's burdens and telling them, "How good and pleasant it is when we live together in unity!" Ultimately I can exclaim the truth, "For there the LORD bestows his blessing, even life forevermore."

We finished hiking the last seven of our sixteen-mile excursion in the dark. Honestly, for me it went faster than any of the other hikes that we had done that week. As we were walking into pitch black, headlamps paving the way, I could not help but wonder what it might have been like had we not been honest with each other and extended grace. We probably would have never even noticed a difference. But with honesty came grace, and now we were able to look past our own strivings and individuality and see others in need of grace like us. During that evening in the Smokey Mountains, with eight of us trekking through a dark and silent night, God really showed us something big. Grace changes everything.

Individual Reflection / Group Discussion

Have you ever had a crisis moment that propelled you toward honesty and community? What was it like?

Is it difficult for you to admit physical/mental/emotional/spiritual weakness? Explain.

Part 3

THOUGHTS ON HONESTY, THE CHURCH, AND SEEING PAST OURSELVES

18

MIRRORS

Stories are like dreams. They have the power to completely take us to another place. This is especially true with fiction. I once heard a preacher say that today is just like in the Old Testament, when kings would dream dreams and prophets would interpret the dreams because the kings had no idea what the visions meant. Today we have people who share stories with us in all kinds of ways (movies, books, person to person, etc.). Many of these are fictional stories, but they point to a greater truth for us to extract. This is one of those stories.

Once upon a time there was a little girl who loved people. In fact, she hardly ever stayed inside of her home because she loved people so much. This little girl loved to ride her bike around town and see all of the people doing different things. Some of the people were shopping, some of them were working, and others were having fun just like her. Many times the little girl would say "hello" to people as she rode her bike on the sidewalks and streets of the town. Most of the time people would say "hi" back to the little girl. This made the little girl feel appreciated and accepted. She loved being noticed by others because it made her feel special, like she mattered to the ones who noticed her. The little girl also loved to notice other people, because she wanted them to feel just as special as she.

Every day the little girl would ride her bike around town and notice people. Often, if she came across someone who needed help she would even stop and help them. Usually, once a week the little girl would help the store clerk carry fruit into his store after a shipment had been unloaded. On another day during the week, she would stop by the local car wash and help whoever was there wash their car. Free of charge of course. If there was ever anyone who really needed a great deal of help that day, the little girl had no problem investing her entire day into that person and helping them. The only stipulation for the little girl, from her parents, was that she be home in time for dinner every evening.

At dinnertime the little girl told her parents about all of the hap-penings that day. She highlighted all of the people whom she had noticed as she was riding her bike and shared how she had helped several of them with their day-to-day obligations. The little girl was always excited to tell her parents about her day, and her parents always smiled back and told her that she was lucky to be so young and free-spirited. This lifestyle of noticing people and taking part in their lives went on for years with the little girl, all the way until she was no longer little anymore. Then she became a teenager.

On her thirteenth birthday, the girl was excited about all of the people who were coming to her party. She had sent out invitations to the entire town, and many people had told her that they would be in attendance. The girl was so excited that she began getting ready for the party early on the morning of her birthday.

As she was getting ready, the girl's mother came into her room with a large rectangular present that had been wrapped in the most beautiful paper. The girl was excited to see what the present was, and so she asked her mother if she might open it early. Her mother agreed and told her that was why she had brought it into the girl's room—so that the present could help her get ready for her birthday party. Eagerly the girl ripped through the wrapping paper and unveiled the shiniest object she had ever seen. It was a large rectangular mirror with a golden frame. The girl marveled at the mirror's beauty and breathlessly thanked her mother, who was closing the bedroom door so that her daughter could continue getting ready in privacy.

As the girl stared into the mirror, in awe of its beauty, she suddenly became terrified. She realized that she was staring directly into her own reflection. Immediately the girl noticed a pimple on her chin and screamed to her mother to borrow some makeup. Then, as quickly as that had occurred, she noticed her hair had not been curled and yelled again for a curler to be brought into her room. This went on for hours. The girl would look into the mirror, notice something about herself she did not like, and desperately try to fix what appeared to be wrong. Eventually, the girl sat on the floor of her bedroom and started sobbing. She knew she could not go to her own birthday party looking the way that she did, and so she decided to hide in her room during the party and hope that no one would notice she was gone.

However, people did notice that the girl was missing her own party. Only a short time had passed since the party began when everyone started questioning where the girl was. After all, this was her birthday party. The girl's mother came back to her daughter's room to find her weeping on her bedroom floor. When asked what was bothering her, the girl told her mother that although it was a thoughtful gift, the mirror had ruined everything. Now all that she could think about was how she looked, and she did not like not being able to notice anybody but herself. "Oh child," the girl's mother said as she ran her fingers through her daughter's hair. "There are so many girls at this party who would be jealous to look like you." The thought proposed by her mother, although disturbing, did make the girl feel a little better. At least she knew she was not the ugliest person at the party. The girl decided to go out and meet her guests.

As the girl walked out to meet everyone at her party, she was thankful that they had come to celebrate with her. The only problem was that although she had talked to her mother earlier, she could not stop thinking about herself and what others thought as they looked at her. Did people think she was beautiful, somewhat attractive, or at least not the worst looking person in the world?

As the years went on, the girl hung the mirror that had been given to her on her wall in her bedroom. As she grew older, the girl stopped riding her bike and exchanged it for a fancy car in the hope that people would stare as she drove down the street. The girl still liked being noticed by others as she did when she was little. However, instead of noticing others first and then being noticed by them in return, the girl hardly ever noticed anyone else . . . unless it was to compare their looks or their cars to her own. Then, as time progressed, the girl became a woman, and eventually the woman died. And no one knew anything about the woman's heart, except that when she was a little girl she noticed people and they noticed her also. No one knew what had made the little girl change so much. No one in the town knew of the mirror that hung on her bedroom wall. She had gone from noticing everyone to seeing only herself.

Individual Reflection / Group Discussion

Have you ever been in a life stage where you could only see yourself? What was it like?

What does an ability to focus on others bring to the life of a Christian?

19

RESCUE

Maybe we want to live in honesty, and maybe we are still afraid of what that means. Maybe we want to not spend all of our time looking in the mirror and trying to fix ourselves, hiding from others, or blaming others in order to make everything feel right; and maybe we have become too comfortable in our own secret lifestyles that change is not an option. Maybe this idea of being naked and unashamed makes sense when it is put into proper perspective, and maybe we are so confused by our own secrets that perspective was thrown out the window a long time ago.

Either way, there is still hope. Either way we must know that whether we are ashamed or unashamed in our current lifestyles, we all have faults, and that means we have the choice to either be humble and honest about it or not. To say it another way: this life is about being transparent with our faults as opposed to being deceptive. Both ways start off the same. Typically individuals or communities look at themselves in the mirror and decide that somewhere along the line they became flawed. The difference comes in how they go about handling this knowledge. People who choose to become honest—taking their gaze away from the mirror—experience grace in their humility, and oftentimes, healing and restoration.

People who embrace deceptiveness tend to hide their imperfections and secrets so that no one else can see.

Honestly, at times we are all deceptive in how we are vulnerable with others. We attempt to cover our faults through consumerism and our use of useless yet elaborate items. We hide from others whom we fear might call out our weaknesses, and we point out other people's failures in order to avoid having any negative attention being put on us. This lifestyle perpetuates a cycle that is far more deceptive than anyone could have ever thought at the beginning. It does not just end with the purchasing of makeup products and the consumption of needless goods, keeping resources out of the hands of orphans and widows. This lifestyle actually blinds us so much so that we cannot see our next-door neighbors. Consumed with becoming the epitome of perfection in everyone else's eyes, we cannot see past our own reflection. We turn our glance away from the needs of others; and ultimately, neglect the hurting, bleeding, starving, and vulnerable people (many of them children) in this world. This is how it all falls apart. This is what we have done.

In order to help unpack this idea, imagine a family with two children, living in a small town. Devin, the father, and his wife, Teresa, work hard to provide for their children, Matt and Sara. Both parents went to college and, before starting a family together, landed solid careers, ensuring financial sustainability for their home. Devin and Teresa both work ten-hour days but are usually home in time for dinner with their children, who are finished with high school extracurricular activities by that time. Because they both work so hard, the family doesn't seem to struggle to pay the bills; and each month there is always extra income to use to go out to eat, go to movies, shop for new things, and have a comfortable financial cushion. The entire family even goes to church every Sunday. From the outside looking in Devin and Teresa have a healthy and happy family.

It would come as a surprise to those who know him that Devin has always had difficulty living in honesty with his wife and children in regard to how he feels inadequate as the spiritual leader of his home. As a result, he presses his family to never miss church, to read their Bibles religiously, and to obsessively shun anything that looks or smells like sin. Likewise, Teresa, not able to be honest about her own feelings of inadequacy, constantly but secretly scrutinizes her physical appearance. She is driven by her pursuit of possessing the best clothes, the most expensive makeup, and fulfilling the most extensive diet and exercise programs. Although this is not directly communicated to their children, Matt and Sara learn the behavior while still young and each day receive more and more engraining of what is taught to be the purpose of a fulfilling life.

Although there seems to be no big secrets within this family's walls, the idea of becoming vulnerable with each other in regard to insecurities and fears has not been brought to the front of any of their minds. Through commercials on television, magazine articles, and conversations with friends, Devin and Teresa have become convinced they can fix these insecurities on their own. For Teresa this could mean engaging in new exercise plans, knowing how to dress for her specific body type, and continually buying what advertisers tell her to buy. In short, she knows the image she should portray, and she knows how to portray it. For Devin, dealing with his insecurities includes a lofty spirituality that few would attempt to attain.

He strives to never miss a day of Bible reading and to achieve sinless perfection. Whether intentionally or not, Devin and Teresa have modeled these behaviors to their children. Sara happily joins her mother on shopping sprees, while Matt is regimented in working on his spiritual life.

The lifestyle portrayed by Devin and Teresa's family is one that most would call a typical Christian American lifestyle. In fact, their home may look like many of our homes. But let's take some time to peel back a few layers of what might really be happening. Let me use Teresa as my prime example, and please allow me to be a bit allegorical for a moment.

Teresa has a longing inside of her to be considered beautiful, and she invests a great deal of energy into fulfilling this longing. In the April issue of her favorite magazine Teresa reads that wearing a red dress will make her more beautiful. So she buys one. Then in the June issue of the same magazine she reads that wearing a purple dress will make her more beautiful. So she buys a purple dress. Then in the July issue, it's a white dress. At the end of these three months Teresa has three new dresses, none of which actually fulfilled her longing to be considered beautiful.

If instead of relying on herself and her own efforts to relieve her insecurities, Teresa decided to become honest about her longing to be considered beautiful, her situation might look something like this: Teresa tells Devin that she longs to be considered beautiful and that she has a hard time believing she is beautiful. In this Teresa is becoming honest and laying herself bare before her husband. Devin then has the opportunity to pour into his wife, telling her how beautiful she is to him, and that his love extends beyond anything a magazine might tell her. Teresa's honesty has been met with grace. Over time, as she continues to live in honesty about these things with her husband, and as her husband continually meets her with grace, they begin to experience deeper fellowship together. Eventually, this fellowship causes Teresa to stop looking in magazines for how to be beautiful, and instead to have her longing fulfilled and her insecurities dissipated by her husband's acceptance of her.

As Teresa begins to realize the deep beauty inside herself, she slowly begins looking for the deep beauty in others. She realizes that in order to love her neighbor as she loves herself,[1] she must first actually love herself. Devin helps her do just that. As Teresa begins to walk in the authority of her newfound confidence and acceptance, she experiences a freedom that she never imagined . . . and she wants others to experience the same freedom.

She begins looking for ways to pour into other people, whether it be having an unusually lengthy conversation with her neighbor outside, volunteering for a young girls summer camp, or teaching her daughter of the value she has in Christ. The more time she spends investing into the lives of others the more Teresa opens herself up to the diversity of people. She now interacts with people in all sorts of life stages, income levels, educational backgrounds, and passions. Teresa begins to deeply care for others no matter how little she has in common with them. She makes friends with people who have needs and she makes friends with other people, like her, who have become passionate about people who have needs.

Without her even realizing it, Teresa has transformed from someone who spends most of her time thinking about herself and improving herself to someone who vigorously works for the freedom, safety, and provision of others. All because she became honest, was met with grace, grew into fellowship, and stretched that fellowship beyond herself and her previous social circle. This story is 1 John 1:7 in action.

Now perhaps this same transformation happens in Devin's life and he too becomes honest about his insecurities as a spiritual leader. Teresa gracefully affirms that Devin, by being himself, is the right spiritual leader for their family. Devin begins affirming his brothers in Christ the way he has been affirmed, and in doing so begins caring for the spiritual needs of others. The transformations of both Devin and Teresa would undoubtedly impact their children in a positive way and potentially trickle down through generations. This family changes from an inwardly focused family to an outwardly focused family. Grace has come with honesty, honesty has brought about fellowship, and their fellowship has extended beyond the walls of their own home.

Suppose this scenario happens to an entire church rather than simply one family of four. Can you imagine the impact on the world?

So when I talk about not shaming homosexuals or being honest about one's own individual struggle with sexuality, or any issue for that matter, what I really want is for people to come together in a place where everyone can be honest. Where everyone, imperfect as we are, can be received with grace. My hope is that we will slowly begin to take our eyes away from the mirror, which has us scrutinizing every little part of our physical and spiritual selves, and instead see others in their most honest places. Because sooner or later, after everything has been laid bare and there are no secrets amongst a community, people will begin to share each other's hopes and dreams. And furthermore, those dreams will arise from the eyes of people who have looked past themselves and seen a world that needs their time, their money, and their life-styles to be honestly seeing it as it is: hurting, dying, and in desperate need of rescue and grace. This is the humble and honest kind of nakedness in action, an honesty that sees the world because it does not stare in the mirror in an attempt to fix itself. In its own honesty, this form of nakedness has received the grace of God, through Jesus, that has accomplished all. This honesty goes out into the streets and alleys, compelling the hurting to come and eat with the Father.

Now let me share my friend's story, a real-life story that closely reflects the allegory of Devin and Teresa's family.

Some years ago I met a man named Pat Bradley. I sat in his office and listened to him open his heart and life to me in a way that I had not experienced in quite some time. After just meeting the man, Pat told me how around twenty-five years previous to our conversation his life was in turmoil. In 1979 Pat was drinking all of the time and literally was about a day away from being homeless and out on the street.

Then Pat told me that he decided to be honest with himself and others, and that God had met him at every level of his honesty with a huge amount of grace. Pat went to ninety Alcoholics Anonymous meetings in ninety days and started learning to live more of a selfless life. He slowly began a lifestyle that allowed him to look past himself and see others in their greatest moments of need. In response to Pat's honesty, God showed him just how much poverty, hunger, lack of medical care, and other social injustices there are in the world.

Some years after having attended his first Alcoholics Anonymous meeting, Pat started taking trips around the world in order to help those in need.

Eventually, he and his wife, Sue, started a nonprofit organization called International Crisis Aid. The organization established four different campaigns in places all over the world that meet people's needs right where they are. International Crisis Aid continues to establish these campaigns in new places all the time. The campaigns are called Food, Health, Home, and Safe, and they provide each of the people who need them with whatever they need at the time. These campaigns have saved thousands upon thousands of lives and continue to do so right now. However, what was incredibly intriguing to me about this conversation with Pat was what was going on with the final campaign, Safe.

Since 2006 International Crisis Aid has been able to establish a multitude of homes for victims of sex trafficking around the world. Crisis Aid's homes are filled with young girls who have been rescued from the horrors of trafficking.[2] To me this is one of the most beautiful reconciliations of all. International Crisis Aid takes girls who may feel used and discarded and lets them know that they are truly beautiful.

Little did I know when I first started talking with Pat that I was sitting in the office of a man who started an organization that has rescued and rehabilitated numerous girls from this evil—more girls than I could have thought possible at the time. And it was all due to the incredible grace of God. As I sat in Pat's office the truth struck me: ninety Alcoholics Anonymous meetings in ninety days. Grace comes with honesty. And grace affects everyone.

Individual Reflection / Group Discussion

Do you feel like you are honest about your own nakedness and imperfection? Why or why not?

Think about Pat's story. How might we learn from his life and move into having a greater impact for Christ in the world?

20

RECONCILIATION

God is in the process of bringing the world back to Himself. We all have a significant longing and motivation inside of us to bring all of who God is into the broken places of this world. We want to be part of what He is doing. This is because God made us and He loves us.

God has always been doing this type of thing . . . bringing people back into His fellowship after we screw it up for one reason or another. Think about the Israelites. They end up going into Egypt's captivity because of their neglect for God, and then He brings them out to freedom. Then they complain so much that they end up wandering around a small desert for forty years, and then God brings them into the Promised Land (see the book of Exodus). He consistently brings us back to Himself again and again, and I am beginning to believe that this is because there is a greater plan in mind. God is working toward redeeming the entire world and establishing His kingdom here through guys like Pat . . . and people like you and me.

In one way this idea is pretty simple. God sent His Son into our world to die for us; and even more than that, to not stay dead for us but rise and live again so we might have a relationship with Him.

He did this so that everything wrong might be restored and so that we can have abundant life. This makes sense to me. But when I think about what this means to the world now, today, I begin to wonder how exactly I am supposed to play a part.

If God really is bringing this world back to Himself, this means that there is power to set free those who are enslaved. If I am living a life that is doing nothing to help wounded people in the world, then there is power for me to get involved. If God really is bringing this world back to Himself today, then He is calling me to take part in this bringing back. He is calling me, like my friend Pat, to look for hurting people and for ways I can partner with them in their lives. He is calling me to look beyond the mirror in my attempt to fix myself every day.

For me, understanding this idea is like understanding water in a flowing brook. I might find it easy enough to place my hands into the water and feel its presence rushing past my skin, but it is another experience for me to actually grasp the water, to pull it out of the stream and witness its grace and power. The idea that God is bringing a fallen world back to Himself must be embraced as truth and not just a general thought. It is a truth so honest that hearing it leaves us either standing in the light through participating with Christ or hiding in darkness and living lives of inconsistency and ignorance.

To be honest with ourselves now is to say that we do, in fact, live lives of inconsistency and ignorance already. This is because we are a fallen people. When given the choice to look to the world around us and see the hurting or look into the mirror and see what culture calls "not enough," we choose to look at ourselves and fill our lives with an excess of anything that poses an empty promise to complete our lives. We are fallen because we are no different from Adam and Eve. We want to be better, we want to be noticed, and we have convinced ourselves that in order to accomplish both of these we need to continually work to become the greatest at whatever it is we desire to do . . . and the best at however it is we desire to do it. This cultural lifestyle has crept into the corners of our minds and kept us looking into the mirror for far too long. All the while the world needs grace, and the simple truth—that God is in the process of bringing this fallen world back to Himself and that we have been invited to participate—to continue to reign free.

The most interesting reality about this invitation is in Luke 14 where Jesus tells a parable about a certain man preparing a great banquet and inviting guests. For the most part, it is not those who are invited first who participate in the actual bringing back of the world to God. Those first invited reject the invitation because they are more worried about what is going on in their own individual lives. Maybe they are climbing the ladder of success, or simply tending their field; but one way or another these people—the first invitees—decline the invitation and leave the one who is doing the inviting to a difficult choice. A difficult choice, but an easy one to make nonetheless. This is when the host diverts from his original plan, and says to his servant, "Go out quickly into the streets and alleys of the town and bring in the poor, the crippled, the blind and the lame" (Luke 14:21). And since the host in the parable stands for God, we can almost hear our Father exclaim to Himself as the servant leaves the room with his specific orders: "These are the ones with whom I will restore my kingdom on earth. These are the ones who will participate in this reconciliation of all humankind. These are the ones whom I will draw to the heart of the kingdom of God."

The difficult part in understanding this invitation lies in the realization that in order to become a participant in such a great calling,
we must become humble and think of ourselves as less. If we think
we are the ones who receive the initial invitation, then we will,
as it says in Luke 14, undoubtedly reject the call. However, if we
choose to acknowledge that we are the crippled ones, that we are
the people who, for the life of us, cannot pull ourselves together,
we can be brought to our Father. We cannot get everything figured out, and we struggle with many things from day to day. But if
we can be honest about the fact that we are ones to whom God
has sent His servant in order to compel us to dine with Him and
take part in what He is doing in the world, then we can take part
in this calling. However, we must admit that we cannot get there on
our own. We need Him. We must acknowledge our brokenness;
and instead of refusing the invitation to participate in this calling
because of our lifestyles, we must allow ourselves to be compelled
by the Great Host and participate in something greater than ourselves. Something that has the potential to set people free, to bring
humanity to a place where we are living lifestyles of difference and
change and hope and honesty. But the greatest of these is honesty.

Individual Reflection / Group Discussion

Take a moment to consider ways you can participate in God's
movement to bring this world back to Himself. What did you come
up with?

When invited, are you more like the first-invited group of Luke 14
or the second-invited group? Explain.

21

PAUL

The apostle Paul wrote an incredible letter to the Galatians. In it he tells them that there is no other gospel than the one he preached to them the last time he visited Galatia. He tells the story of how this gospel saved his life, gave him new spiritual awareness, and allowed him to become an "apostle—sent not from men nor by a man, but by Jesus Christ and God the Father, who raised him from the dead. . . ."[1]

This letter is truly amazing. Paul confronts Christians about the huge difference between living under the law and living under grace. He explains freedom as something that exists simply because it is good that it exists, and that we are intended to experience it for freedom's sake alone.[2] Paul exhorts the Galatians about allowing themselves to be circumcised after receiving Christ, or even thinking about allowing themselves to be circumcised. He writes, "You foolish Galatians! Who has bewitched you? Before your very eyes Jesus Christ was clearly portrayed as crucified. I would like to learn just one thing from you: Did you receive the Spirit by the works of the law, or by believing what you heard?"[3]

I love this letter. It begins with grace. It ends with grace. And even though I read it in my little blue NIV, I can almost imagine how large Paul's handwriting must have been when he wrote, "See what large letters I use as I write to you with my own hand!"[4] Paul was undoubtedly a man of passion, and he must have been a man with confidence. Even more than that, I do believe that the gospel of Jesus Christ was so close to his heart that when any church began to head in the wrong direction—especially in regard to an understanding of ministry, grace, or even truth itself—they surely received a first-class letter in the mail.

My thoughts led me to wonder what kind of letter the church of North America might receive if Paul was still around today. Maybe it would be something like this:

> Paul, an apostle of Christ, to the church of North America. You self-centered Americans! What on earth are you doing? I wish that I could come to you now and teach you the truth once again. Church ministry has nothing to do with the size of your church. The gospel is about people. Growth does not mean that your local body has voted to build an addition larger than the local YMCA. Are you trying to be attractive like the world? Are you so ignorant that you have not noticed yourselves acting exactly like the people you see in the media every day? Why must you always try to be the best at everything you do? Why does your church have to be the biggest and most elaborate? Why?

> Some of you do not strive to become big in numbers, yet you strive to become the most doctrinally

sound and traditionally right in your communities. I would love for the hurting of your communities to be able to come and attend your services without feeling ostracized, but you have done nothing to set yourselves apart as churches operating under God's grace!

You have raced to become the fastest growing, and in turn only ended up with the biggest building. Even many smaller communities are striving to be just like the bigger ones. You have left the heart of the gospel that desires no one to be in need in its community, and you have created the need to fit in, the need to be wealthy, and the need to appear okay. I beg you with this pen that is in my hand as I write these words. Remember the gospel to which you were called. Remember the places from which you were called and return to the place that seeks to bring God's kingdom to earth. Return to the place that renders everyone staring into the face of grace, not having to prove themselves a saint. Return to the freedom of Christ, for the sake of the freedom of Christ.

Know that it is God who causes us to be firm in Christ. Know that we are called to participate in the gospel of Jesus Christ, not as only hearers, but as those who wrap their lifestyles around the things that God wants to accomplish with this world and His people. May we know that it is by His grace that we do these things.

No matter how reading that fictitious letter might make you feel, I hope we can agree that the church is self-obsessed, with an obvious inability to see the world. We have looked at our own bodies and believed we are screwed up, mainly because at some point we tried to elevate ourselves, even if just in our own imaginations. From any form of struggle conceivable, there is a great temptation to live in secret and preserve ourselves from potential outside ridicule. The reality is that many times there is no true community in which to live honestly. And because of this, we either have become fakers in the church or cynics who criticize the church from the bleachers.

The bottom line—where all of these ideas (regarding honesty, the church, and seeing past ourselves) fall together—is that God initially created this world beautifully. Everything was beautiful and everything was honest. From geography to weather patterns, from relationships to the way these relationships relate, from a simple handshake to sex itself. God made everything in this world beautiful. But sin came and twisted everything into an incredibly deceptive knot. We can see glimpses of beauty in the world today, but many things are ultimately tainted with a darkness that attempts to take the focus off of God. Even many of our churches have adopted a twisted form of ministry and have used it to become famous. This fame can come from elaborate amenities, political "rightness," and even seemingly flawless doctrine. All of this is a form of staring in the mirror. We make ourselves look as good as possible and miss out on everyone and everything around us. We can see only ourselves.

We see many people who claim to follow the gospel of Jesus instead pursuing the biggest buildings, the most compelling shows, and the most appealing church "experience" one can assemble. This kind of church feels more like cinema, meeting our desire to be entertained, but failing to become a place that meets hurting people's needs. It is dangerous to claim goodness in all of this excess . . . especially when there are so many neglected people in the world who are praying that someone with resources comes to them. I know that the temple of God was elaborate in the Old Testament, but today God has changed what the temple actually is. We are the temple.[5] God is in us. And He wants us to go into the gutters and compel others to meet with Him.

When I think of the movie *Schindler's List*, I remember a scene near the end when, after he has rescued a large multitude of people from death camps, Schindler is looking through all of his belongings. He is saying to himself that he could have sold his watch and rescued one more. He seems to frantically pick up items and question whether or not he has fulfilled the purpose of what he was called to do. When I think about that scene in the movie I think about walking into my own home, or any number of church buildings in North America. I look around, finally considering how many starving people there are in the world. I might consider the number of children who have been enslaved and not given the opportunity to live a fulfilling life. And then I might think about just how much money I, and others, have invested into whatever it was that we have been defining as ministry. These thoughts are incredibly humbling to me; and I know that I, along with the North American church of God, have an exceedingly long way to go in changing my lifestyle to one that Jesus has called me to live.

Individual Reflection / Group Discussion

What do you think of Paul's fictitious letter to the church of North America?

What are some ways you and the church can alter your lifestyles to better impact this world for Christ?

22

THE GOOD NEWS

Somewhere along the lines of church and ministry we got the idea that we could not tell others how hard life actually is. We could not share our deepest struggles. And if we did we were usually met with some kind of formulaic approach to get better. And we didn't realize we were modeling this lifestyle for our children. In the midst of all this striving to show ourselves as perfect people, good enough to worship God in the pew next to our neighbor, we forgot about grace. We forgot about grace, and we forgot that grace comes with honesty; and that if we are ever to experience the freedom that Christ and His grace can bring to us, then we must lay ourselves bare before God and each other. We must take the risk of being known in the midst of our failures, and we must no longer claim, even if it is only with our lifestyles, to be without sin.

When I initially wrote Paul's fictitious letter to the church of North America, I knew that in a lot of senses it would be taken the wrong way. I knew that people would immediately turn on their defenses and ask the question, "Who are you to say such things, to ask such pointed questions?" I am sure that many of those people may have stopped reading at that point, and I understand if they did. But the other day, I was talking with an engineer friend of mine, and he said that engineers have the tendency to look at everything and ask the following three questions: "What is the device I am looking at intended to do? Is it accomplishing its purpose? Are there needless parts of this apparatus that can be removed and in doing so potentially cause it to run more efficiently?"

To be honest, I have been asking these questions a lot lately in regard to the church. I read the book of Acts and although I am not seeking an ecclesiological explanation as to whether or not we are to be that exact church today, I do ask myself what the church of God is intended to do. I read Acts, and I see a spreading of the gospel and a place where no one is in need, and I know that this is not our church today. We do attempt to spread the gospel, but in many ways we have redefined what "gospel" is so much so that we do not associate it with making sacrificial offerings of our time, money, and lifestyles so that others may know Jesus. Instead, the "gospel" has become a glorified get-out-of-hell-free card and an instruction booklet for how to live the "right" sort of life. Finally I ask myself, are there needless parts of the church that we might remove and in so doing, meet the world at a greater level than we might have thought before? Can we be better stewards of our time, money, and lifestyles, and can we be more efficient for the kingdom of God in this world? I believe we can. I believe it begins with honesty.

And if these ideas are not enough to make us wonder about the efficiency of the church today, maybe the book of Amos will help. Amos was a prophet, and he shared the following message from God:

> I can't stand your religious meetings.
>   I'm fed up with your conferences and
>   conventions.

I want nothing to do with your religion projects,
    your pretentious slogans and goals.
I'm sick of your fund-raising schemes,
    your public relations and image making.
I've had all I can take of your noisy ego-music.
    When was the last time you sang to me?
Do you know what I want?
    I want justice—oceans of it.
I want fairness—rivers of it.
    That's what I want. That's all I want.[1]

We need to take an honest look at ourselves and how we are taking part with God in bringing this world back to Himself. If we have neglected to participate in this calling because lifestyle changes seem to be too difficult, then we must know that we have silently given permission for a lack of honesty, and as a result, a lack of community to run rampant and destroy our neighbors.

To sum all this up, the church (especially today) is not a place where honesty is gracefully accepted; and because of this lack of honesty and grace, people do not bring their whole hearts to church. Because people do not bring their whole hearts to church, the church has become blind and cannot *honestly* see the hurting of this world in their misery: Naked, Starving, Thirsty, Vulnerable, and Abused. Why? Because we cannot see past ourselves. We cannot stop looking into the mirror. We try to make ourselves the biggest and the best. And when we fail at that, we sew fig leaves to appear to be okay. We learn to hide from each other, and we learn to blame. And while we become more and more injured by our secrets and choices to avoid the light of honest living, the people who could really use our time, resources for survival, and the hope of abundant life, fall by the wayside.

But the good news is that Jesus came and died for all of this. And because He didn't stay dead, we don't have to either. We can live in grace and bring it to the world. It is possible. Because of Christ it is possible. We no longer need to strive to become perfect. We can live under the umbrella of God's grace. Jesus was the perfect one. He accomplished what we could not, so that we might live in freedom and sacrificial love toward others. All He asks is that we confess our need for Him, receive His grace, and give His grace to those who need it most.

Individual Reflection / Group Discussion

Is it possible to look at our own lives and the church like an engineer and remove needless parts? If so, how might we do this? What might need removal?

How can the church bring "oceans of justice" and "rivers of fairness" to this world?

23

FLUSHING OUR SYSTEMS

Flushing our systems of the patterns and processes by which the world entices us to live deceptively must become a priority. Romans 12:2 calls us to "not conform to the pattern of this world, but be transformed by the renewing of your mind." We need to think differently—about ourselves, about each other, about everything. This is the point of the gospel. We need to let God flush our systems of the patterns in this world before it is too late and we no longer can see past our own reflections.

The culture we live in is consumeristic, in that consuming is precisely what we do. We work so that we can purchase, so that we can look better, so that we can consume more, so that we can be better. It all started in the garden of Eden, the moment Adam and Eve believed that they needed to fix themselves, when the deceiving voice told them the obvious half-truth—that they were naked, and that naked, they were not enough. The message of "not good enough" has wreaked havoc on lives and families. However, the good news is that there truly is hope. God really is in the process of bringing this world back to Himself, and He is using people like you and me.

As Adam and Eve felt shame for their nakedness, the beauty of sex also experienced a perversion. For some of us who have been wounded by sexual abuse or the repercussions thereof, God has invited us to help restore the sexuality of the broken and tattered, the weak and the wounded, the little children who have been prohibited from coming freely to Jesus' side. This is one way I believe God has called Christians to get involved with His bringing this world back to Himself. If God has brought us back to Himself through Jesus, then we must also go out into the streets and compel those who cannot come on their own. We must bring them to safety. This is the gospel.

When I think about little children coming to Jesus and the disciples prohibiting them from sitting at His feet, I do not think about those children being trafficked instead of getting to experience the peace of Christ. I do not think of a little girl being forced to have sex with a forty-year-old man instead of embracing the knowledge that God truly does have a plan for her life, one that is vastly different from the evil reality she has known. But when I put it like that—using the words that I just have—I know that I probably should be honest with myself and think of letting the little children come to Jesus in this way. Maybe instead of simply standing back and not getting in the way, Jesus is calling me to actually take a proactive approach and make it possible for children, who otherwise would know no other life than the hell in which they live every day, to come to Jesus' side and experience glimpses of heaven in the beauty of open and honest relationships within community.

To be rescued from a place of loneliness, abandonment, pain, and shame, and to be brought into a place where people care more about each other's well-being than they do their own is definitely a taste of heaven. This is a place where people will help children approach the throne of grace with all of the pain that one little life has had to carry, and then lift them up to experience hope. This is a place where relationship and living in the light overcomes darkness, and this is a place where no child should be kept from entering. I am thankful for people, like my friend Pat Bradley, who instead of neglecting these children in ignorance, have helped them come to Jesus freely. This is an honesty that sees beyond self.

Individual Reflection / Group Discussion

What are some cultural patterns in your life—not necessarily specific sins—that God might want to transform?

How can our understanding of how God views children impact the way we see children all over the world?

24

CLICK

Consider the click of a television remote. It sounds like this:
Sometimes people matter

        to us

            and other times

they do not.

  Usually, if we can see them, people have the potential to matter

           at least a little bit.

But more than likely, if they are out of our sight

      people are usually

        out of our minds.

The other day I saw a little girl on the television. She was starving. Her stomach was bloated and she didn't have any clothes. I didn't know her name and the injustice was too difficult to witness.

        So . . .

I changed the channel.

Changing the channel is Absurdity.

People matter.

People on television are the same as those not on television.

People who are starving are the same as those not starving.

People who are different from me are the same as me.

Human beings are worth the greatest sacrifice, the greatest gift, and the greatest life.

People are worth my greatest sacrifice.

If Jesus sacrificed for me,

I can sacrifice for people.

If Jesus died for me,

I can die for people.

Or . . .

I can change the channel.

Click.

Click.

We cannot keep changing the channel. When given the choice to be honest about ourselves, our lives, and our weaknesses, we cannot run in fear of what others might think of us. If we do we silently give ourselves permission to not be honest with our Christian communities about what is going on in the world and how we might participate in what God is calling us to do. There comes a point in all of our lives where we look at ourselves and we start thinking about all of the things in which we have invested. At the same time we look at the world and we see how much God wants us to participate with Him in bringing His kingdom to this place. My hope is that we take an honest look at ourselves, and the grace of God, and that we choose to participate in His calling before it is too late. This is a calling to live in the light, both individually and as church communities. This is a calling to take our eyes off the mirror and see a world that needs the grace of God through Jesus. This is a calling to change our lifestyles so we can better take part in what God is doing. This is a calling that demands all of who we are, not just a church missions budget, not just a tithe. This calling demands our life and a lifestyle that embraces the gospel of Jesus Christ.

Individual Reflection / Group Discussion

What are some ways you figuratively *change the channel*? How can we learn to *stop changing the channel*?

What are some ways our own values can get in the way of helping others?

25

NEW ORLEANS

A few years ago I led a team of college students to New Orleans in order to help clean up some of the mess from Hurricane Katrina. When we arrived we were shocked by the disparity in New Orleans at the time. There were incredibly wealthy areas that were quickly up and running shortly after the hurricane went through; and there were impoverished parts that, years later, had not even been touched by human hands. At one point on our trip a member of our team came up to me and asked if we might make peanut butter and jelly sandwiches and hand them out to homeless people as we passed by them on the street. My initial reaction was that this was a good idea, but after further discussion we decided that the hurting people of New Orleans did not want our peanut butter and jelly sandwiches. They wanted our lives.

Ultimately, I did not want the members of our team to fall into the habit of good deeds and fuzzy feelings that so often entrap many Christians. We give away some trinket of good cheer or make a small sacrifice that may meet someone's needs for a moment, and then we walk away feeling as though we have saved the world. A short time later, after we had arrived back from our trip, one of our team members made a bold move. She packed up and headed down to New Orleans for the next couple of years. Then it hit me. God was demanding my lifestyle in the same way he was calling my friend. Today I see Him doing the same exact thing. The only difference is now I know that I honestly have a choice. I will either be the person who rejects this honest invitation because I have better things to do and feel that I have already done my good deed, or I will be the one who allows God to compel me to come and take part in His kingdom. A kingdom of difference and change.

Part of living a dishonest lifestyle comes with the belief that we can be part of a short-term missions team or a one-time charitable experience, and as a result, live our lives feeling as though we have truly made a positive impact on the world. Through living in the light we can learn to embrace the hurting of the world rather than ignore them by using temporary Band-Aid solutions. We are not called to quick fixes.

Individual Reflection / Group Discussion

What does it look like to give someone your life versus giving them a momentary charitable experience?

How have you been impacted by someone giving their life to you versus helping you one time?

26

YOKE

So Jesus said, "My yoke is easy and my burden is light,"[1] and we are supposed to somehow wrap our lives around this concept and then become powerful members of the kingdom of God. I am quite confident that He was not talking solely about oxen. We can know through context that this analogy touches on farming. Jesus used several farming analogies throughout Scripture, and the yoke was the big wooden thing you put on the back of your animals in order to pull a plow. Simply put, the yoke connected everything—the animals to each other and to the plow. Without the yoke, a person might just have a couple of oxen and a plow, but nothing to make them work together. And ultimately, this gets nothing accomplished when one is trying to prepare soil for planting.

This brings me to another point: the plow, connected to the oxen through the yoke and other parts, was what helped make the soil good for planting. Jesus spends quite a bit of time discussing soil in Matthew 13, and we know from His words that it is imperative for us to become good soil. If this happens, then when God plants something true in our lives, it sticks and produces something greater in the long run.

But the yoke is what brought all of this together. It's the glue. Without it, everything is its own separate entity; but with the yoke, everything becomes one. So what is the yoke? Simple, it is God's words, His truth for us, what He wants to teach us. And the first thing that Jesus wants us to know about what He wants to teach us is that His teachings are easy and light. Not hard and heavy, weighed down with tons of theological rhetoric or philosophical ideals. Jesus' teaching for us is a way to live. For His disciples and followers during the time Jesus walked the earth, His yoke was a way to live that did not embrace the hierarchies and religious checklists (sewing, hiding, and blaming) of the Pharisees and other religious leaders. For us today, I believe that Jesus' yoke is very much the same as it was then. However, I believe that the yoke of Jesus can accomplish so much more than we allow.

Many times the church bombards us with lists of what is necessary to become good Christians. We write those lists down, we take them home, and we wrap our lifestyles around these teachings. It is almost as if every single morning we wake up, we stare at ourselves in the mirror, and we ask, "What else can I do to be a better Christian?"

When we fail at our strivings, we feel incredible amounts of guilt. In response, we sew figurative fig leaves to cover our failings, we hide, we blame, and we make our lists longer and more difficult, hoping that somehow we can get to the place where we are worthy to worship with other Christians around us.

Even when we are away from the church, we strive so hard to be successful. We do not claim to worship the dollar, but our lifestyles seem to be wrapped around its influence and power over us. All the while Jesus has told us that His yoke is easy and that His burden is light, but our lives do not match up with what Jesus is saying to us.

The honest truth is that we cannot climb high enough to reach a point of success where we become content. In the same way, we cannot attain levels of spirituality through fulfilling checklists other people create for us. There is nothing we can do to come into the place that only the grace of God can bring us. Except be honest.

Grace comes with honesty, and because of this, Jesus' teaching is easy and His burden is light. We can now become honest with ourselves. We can become honest within our church communities. We can stop trying to make ourselves perfect through keeping secrets and wearing elaborate Christian outfits. We can together become honest with each other and God and choose to embrace a world that is hurting, starving, thirsty, naked, and in desperate need of intervention. Ultimately, we can stop using our lifestyles, time, and resources to further burden ourselves with the overwhelming temptation to want more, to have more, and to become more. We can take our faces out of the mirror and instead give our lives to a yoke that is easy and a burden that is light.

This is a yoke that wants no one to go hungry. This is a burden that does not require us to pile more and more rules upon ourselves. This is a yoke that offers grace for everyone. This is a burden that leaves no one in want. This is a yoke that finds us when everyone else has told us that we do not measure up, and lets who we are—because of the grace of God—be enough. This is a burden that only carries the burdens of others and not our own. This is a grace that comes with honesty . . . that opens a fellowship . . . which equals freedom . . . that inspires us to love the world in the same way God loves the world. This is a lifestyle Jesus has called us to live. A lifestyle of honesty. A lifestyle of grace. A lifestyle of fellowship. A lifestyle of freedom from the burdens of our own selfishness, secrets, and shame.

Individual Reflection / Group Discussion

What are some ways you, individually, can align yourself with what God is doing in this world?

What are some ways the church can align itself with what God is doing in this world?

Epilogue

HONESTY AND THE ART OF NARNIA

Some of the most profound and insightful Christian principles come from The Chronicles of Narnia by C. S. Lewis. When I was in college I was jokingly told that if I quoted C. S. Lewis in an argument, I would automatically win any debate in which I was participating.

Honestly, there is something exhilarating about the truths that lie within the pages of this seven-book series. It is almost as if C. S. Lewis had help from God as he was writing these stories, and I am sure he did.

There is one specific quote I want to leave you with that I hope will bring us together and challenge us to live in the light with others who may help us on our journeys.

To some this quote speaks of God. To others the words touch on truth, and wisdom, and love. When I read it I think about honesty: what it is, what it does, and what it is capable of accomplishing in our lives by the power of the Holy Spirit. I cannot help but revel in the potential of grace in our lives and how transformative it can be, if we could simply trust it for what it is: the grace of God through

Jesus Christ. May we know that God desires for us to embrace an honesty that moves us into grace, a grace that moves us into fellowship, and a fellowship that moves us into definitions of freedom that we previously did not even know existed.

As Mr. and Mrs. Beaver put it in *The Lion, the Witch, and the Wardrobe*:

> "If there's anyone who can appear before Aslan without their knees knocking, they're either braver than most or else just silly."
>
> "Then he isn't safe?" said Lucy.
>
> "Safe?" said Mr. Beaver; "don't you hear what Mrs. Beaver tells you? Who said anything about safe? 'Course he isn't safe. But he's good. . . ."[1]

Like Aslan, or God, honesty isn't safe. But it's good.

May we find it now.

NOTES

Prologue: Homeless in the Park
  1. Matthew 25:45.
  2. See Proverbs 24:26.

Chapter 1: Like a Kiss on the Lips
  1. Jesus said, "I have come that they may have life, and have it to the full" (John 10:10).

Chapter 2: Self-Protection
  1. I Corinthians 10:13.
  2. Romans 7:15–19.
  3. See Matthew 7:1–5.
  4. John Burke, *Soul Revolution: How Imperfect People Become All God Intended* (Grand Rapids: Zondervan, 2008), 110.

Chapter 3: Sewing, Hiding, and Blaming
  1. I cover these concepts in more detail in my first book, *Remembering a Forgotten Grace: Thoughts on Shame, Beauty, Romance, and Radiance* (Pasadena, CA: Hope Publishing House, 2008).
  2. Margery Williams, *The Velveteen Rabbit*, illustr. William Nicholson (New York: George H. Doran, 1922), 12–13. Available

online with illustrations at http://digital.library.upenn.edu/wom en/williams/rabbit/rabbit.html.

Chapter 4: Knowing and Being Known
1. Genesis 3:1; 1 Chronicles 21:1; Matthew 4:1; John 10:10.
2. Genesis 1:26.
3. Interestingly, the Greek word for "know," used in John 8:32, is *ginōskō*. An accepted definition of this word in some contexts is "to have sexual relations" (as it is in Matthew 1:25 or Luke 1:34), which in such passages renders in Greek the Hebrew idea of *yada*, to know through sexual intercourse (see Genesis 4:1). I find it intriguing that Jesus would communicate the idea of us knowing "the truth" with a word capable of such intimate meaning. To me this reflects an openness and honesty in relation to God that is best understood through marriage.
4. Psalm 139:23–24.

Chapter 5: Alcoholics Anonymous
1. For references to God as the Beginning and the End, see Revelation 1:8; 21:6; 22:13.
2. Bob Smith and Bill Wilson, *Alcoholics Anonymous: The Story of How Many Thousands of Men and Women Have Recovered from Alcoholism*, 3rd ed. (New York: Alcoholics Anonymous World Services, 1976), 58.

Chapter 6: Darkness and Light
1. 1 John 1:10.
2. James Dobson and Ted Bundy, *Fatal Addiction: Ted Bundy's Final Interview*, interviewed January 23, 1989 (Colorado Springs, CO: Focus on the Family Films, 1989), videocassette (VHS), 56 min. Bundy was put to death in the electric chair at Florida

State Prison on January 24, 1989.

3. For further information about how pornography can lead to violence toward women, visit Hope for the Voiceless (HFTV) at www.hopeforthevoiceless.org.

Chapter 7: "At Least I'm Not . . ."
  1. See Romans 3:21–28; 8:38–39.

Chapter 8: Honest Community
  1. For more information, visit www.xxxchurch.com.
  2. 1 Corinthians 3:10–15.

Chapter 10: Fellowship Equals Freedom
  1. Galatians 5:1.
  2. 1 Corinthians 10:13 says, "No temptation has overtaken you except what is common to mankind." Shame tells us we are the only one.
  3. See 1 John 1:7.
  4. See Romans 12:2.

Chapter 12: The Church and Homosexuality
  1. Lawrence Goldstone and Nancy Goldstone, *Out of the Flames: The Remarkable Story of a Fearless Scholar, a Fatal Heresy, and One of the Rarest Books in the World* (New York: Broadway Books, 2002), 321.
  2. I am aware of many various sexual orientations, including lesbian, gay, bisexual, transgendered, and others. For the purpose of this book, I have chosen to use the word "homosexual" in a more inclusive manner, rather than use the acronym LGBT. This is for simplicity and is not meant as a stereotype or label.
  3. See 1 Corinthians 6:9–10; Galatians 5:19–21; Colossians 3:5–9.

4. "Chastity and Homosexuality" from Catechism of the Catholic Church, accessed October 16, 2013, http://www.vatican.va/archive/ccc_css/archive/catechism/p3s2c2a6.htm#2351.

5. "Sexuality" from SBC.net, the official website of the Southern Baptist Convention, accessed October 16, 2013, http://www.sbc.net/aboutus/pssexuality.asp.

6. Mark A. Yarhouse, *Homosexuality and the Christian: A Guide for Parents, Pastors, and Friends* (Bloomington, MN: Bethany House Publishers, 2010), 26–28.

7. Romans 1:18–27.

8. For the tie-in of the mission of God with Romans 9–11, see the bookends: 1:1–6 and 16:25–27.

9. First Corinthians 5 deals with removing people from Christian fellowship in response to various forms of immorality. It is important to note that Paul had an ongoing relationship with the church of Corinth and continually worked with them to improve their unhealthy community. Through the writing of two separate letters he addressed a group of people who have since become known for all of their dysfunction and lack of respect for God's institution of the church. It is important not to take these specific instructions out of historical context and apply them as blanket statements to our individual situations.

10. See 1 Corinthians 6:18.

Chapter 13: Communal Honesty and Intimacy
    1. Romans 8:1.

Chapter 14: Roadblocks
    1. Mark 10:17–22.
    2. Isaiah 6:1–8.

Chapter 15: Being a Safe Place

1. Karl Marx, "Theses on Feuerbach" (1845) in *Karl Marx and Fredrick Engels Selected Works*, vol. 1; these words are also engraved upon his tombstone.

2. See *The Oxford Dictionary of the Christian Church*, 3rd ed. rev., ed. F. L. Cross and E. A. Livingstone (Oxford: Oxford University Press, 2005), s.vv. "Luther, Martin," "Calvin, John," "Anabaptists," "Zwingli, Ulrich," "Mennonites," "Amish," "Henry VIII," "Wesley, John," "Smyth, John."

3. See Matthew 25:31–46.

4. See 1 John 4:10.

5. 1 Timothy 1:15–16.

Chapter 16: Why Honesty Matters

1. "For the love of money is a root of all kinds of evil. Some people, eager for money, have wandered from the faith and pierced themselves with many griefs" (1 Timothy 6:10).

2. Thinking about the above scenario opens a greater discussion: Does honesty about global needs always trump beauty and comfort? In response to this question, I must respond a bit tongue in cheek: is relationship with Christ and others more important than making ourselves or our communities look good externally? Jesus says that whatever we do for the least of those whom we encounter we do for Him, and He points to the idea that this is how He knows us. So in that case, relationship is more important.

3. A continued scenario: These children can now hear the gospel of Jesus because of the intimate relationships being built between two totally different communities that decided to be honest with each other. The orphanage presented its need (honesty about shortcomings) and received abundance from

a church on the other side of the world. The church saw the orphanage in desperate need of partnership, relationship, and money, and then met those needs with abundance (honesty with themselves in regard to God's calling). In this situation, both kinds of honesty are met with a great measure of grace.

Chapter 19: Rescue
    1. See Mark 12:31.
    2. For more information, visit International Crisis Aid (ICA) at www.crisisaid.org.

Chapter 21: Paul
    1. Galatians 1:1.
    2. See Galatians 5:1.
    3. Galatians 3:1–2.
    4. Galatians 6:11.
    5. See 1 Corinthians 6:19.

Chapter 22: The Good News
    1. Amos 5:21–24 (MSG).

Chapter 26: Yoke
    1. Matthew 11:30.

Epilogue: Honesty and the Art of Narnia
    1. C. S. Lewis, *The Lion, the Witch, and the Wardrobe* (New York: HarperCollins, 1978), 80.

ABOUT THE AUTHOR

A communicator, church planter, idea maker, and storyteller, Rod Tucker is the founding pastor of The River:pm and author of *Remembering a Forgotten Grace: Thoughts on Shame, Beauty, Romance, and Radiance*. Growing up attending Alcoholics Anonymous meetings with his parents instilled in Rod the necessity of honesty, the urgency of grace, and the beauty of community. Through books, speaking, and various forms of media, he seeks to open conversations with real people who are pursuing a real God. Rod and his wife, Anna, live in Kalamazoo, Michigan, where they enjoy listening to, watching, reading, and telling all kinds of stories. To get in touch with Rod or to see what is happening, visit rodtuckersays.com.